BENEATH
THE
SURFACE

BENEATH
THE
SURFACE

STEERING CLEAR OF THE DANGERS
THAT COULD LEAVE YOU SHIPWRECKED

FOREWORD BY JOHN MAXWELL

BOB RECCORD

BROADMAN
&HOLMAN
PUBLISHERS

NASHVILLE, TENNESSEE

0–8054–2568–3

Published by Broadman & Holman Publishers
Nashville, Tennessee

Dewey Decimal Classification: 248
Subject Heading: SEX

Unless otherwise noted, Scripture quotations are from the Holy Bible,
New International Version, copyright © 1973, 1978, 1984 by
International Bible Society. Scripture quotations marked NLT are taken
from the Holy Bible, New Living Translation, copyright © 1996. Used by
permission of Tyndale House Publishers, Inc., Wheaton, Illinois 60189.
All rights reserved.

Library of Congress Cataloging-in-Publication Data

Reccord, Robert E.
    Beneath the surface : steering clear of the dangers that
could leave you shipwrecked / Bob Reccord.
        p.   cm.
    ISBN 0–8054–2568–3
    1. Sex—Religious aspects—Christianity. 2. Temptation.
3. Evangelists—Sexual behavior. I. Title.
    BT708 .R414 2002
    248.4'861—dc21
                                                        2001043374
            5 6 7 8 9 10 06 05 04 03 02

Few messages have stirred my heart and caused me to raise my spiritual and moral guard like Bob Reccord's message in *Beneath the Surface: Steering Clear of the Dangers That Could Leave You Shipwrecked*. I believe that every man and woman needs to read again the standard of God's Word that we might finish faithful and this book will help do that in your life. In its challenges and in the cause it represents, it is a must for your reading.

—Johnny Hunt, Pastor
First Baptist Church, Woodstock, GA

Powerful! Profound! This book has the potential to salvage a sinking man, woman, or couple. If only the *Titanic* had had Bob Reccord at the helm!

June Hunt, President
Hope for the Heart

Through the activities of two well-known men in the Bible—David and Joseph—Bob Reccord allows us to look inside our own lives to view the dangers that await us . . . but also to experience the power that sustains us . . . the power to make the right choice.

H. B. London Jr., Vice President
Ministry Outreach/Pastoral Ministries
Focus on the Family

MAYDAY! . . . MAYDAY! . . . MAYDAY! Marriages are in trouble at an alarming rate! They are being attacked, shot at, rocked from side to side, and many are about to go under. However, just in the nick of time, help is on the way. In his powerful and timely book, *Beneath the Surface: Steering Clear of the Dangers That Could Leave You Shipwrecked,* Dr. Bob Reccord gives some timely and practical advice that can get any marriage back on course. Read it and apply it so that your marriage can have smooth sailing!

—Fred Luter Jr., Senior Pastor
Franklin Avenue Baptist Church, New Orleans, LA

Thank God for Bob Reccord. *Beneath the Surface* is one of the first great spiritual helps for the twenty-first century. The best way to avoid the tragedy of a spiritual shipwreck in the lives of our children, our marriage, and our walk with Jesus is to head it off before it ever happens. *Beneath the Surface* is a cultural guide for spiritually healthy relationships and families . . . every person ought to read it.

—Josh McDowell
Author, *More Than a Carpenter*

This book cuts like a scalpel into the inner sanctum of your soul and then, suddenly, you feel healing flow forth. Highly recommended.

—Patrick Morley
Author, *Man in the Mirror*

In Beneath the Surface, Bob Reccord reminds us of the real Truth that is unsinkable. He throws out the lifeline of marriage and what we do to make the husband-wife bond become the foundation for a Christian family.

—Mary Manz Simon, author and host
Front Porch Parenting radio program

In *Beneath the Surface,* my friend Bob Reccord gives practical advice to those of us who are committed to protecting the relationships we cherish most. It is advice worth heeding.

—Andy Stanley, Pastor
North Point Community Church, Alpharetta, GA

Like a lighthouse on the sea, Bob's book sounds a warning and sets the course for couples who want to avoid the icebergs and set their sails toward a growing and fulfilling marriage.

—Joe Stowell, President
Moody Bible Institute

If there's one thing I've learned, it's that life-saving solutions can come in small vessels. Here's one for those who are serious about staying afloat in the murky waters of today's culture and its hidden dangers to marriage. Be sure to read it and finish well.

—Bruce Wilkinson, Founder and President
Walk Thru the Bible Ministries
Author, *The Prayer of Jabez* and *Secrets of the Vine*

hope that is found in Christ Jesus, the captian of our souls.

—Janet Parshall, host
Syndicated talk-show *Janet Parshall's America*

When Bob Reccord came to Southeastern Baptist Theological Seminary and delivered the essence of this book's message to our students, I thanked God that tomorrow's ministers had the opportunity to hear a challenge such as this. Every future pastor and staff member, missionary and evangelist needs to read this book. Pastor, give it to every young man and woman in your church.

—Paige Patterson, President
Southeastern Baptist Theological Seminary
Wake Forest, NC

Dr. Reccord gives us a divine and practical strategy for avoiding the "icebergs" of immorality that will destroy your life and ministry. While the enemy is busy deceiving countless men and women of influence, this book will give you the courage and hope to finish strong. Every man should read this book!

—Dennis Rainey
Executive Director, FamilyLife

Today's moral mindscape is cluttered with diluted messages, as time-starved men and women struggle to sustain healthy relationships. Dr. Reccord gives a blueprint to renew, revive, and reclaim marriage for the twenty-first century. He bridges the gap between what we say about

Dedication

Dedicated to two very special women in my life.

First, to my Mom, Ruth, who I watched make a marriage work, even when it wasn't easy, and who modeled loyalty and commitment in relationships.

Second, to my precious wife, Cheryl, who has walked with me for almost thirty years and has been a great partner, lover, explorer, and listener. Thanks for making it a great journey!

Acknowledgments

Like most creative projects, books are rarely the work of only one person.

Three people whose help I sought are Carolyn Curtis, Gwen Mitchell, and Sealy Yates. Others too numerous to name provided insight, encouragement, and much-needed prayer support.

But the ones who deserve the utmost thanks are those people who lived through the moral failures described

xii   BENEATH THE SURFACE

in this book and who shared with such trust and openness that I was able to understand how the tragedies they experienced left them reeling with emotional and spiritual shrapnel. In some cases the people who allowed me to tell their stories were the ones who fell; others were their victims. What always characterized their stories were the hurt and devastation they described and the ripple effect they witnessed in the lives of their loved ones. Because of their candor and courage, we can learn from them and be on guard for the dangers that lurked beneath the surface of their lives and eventually shipwrecked them.

Contents

Foreword

I remember the days when affairs, divorces, broken families, and other consequences of moral failures were heard about but not seen. Things like these happened to people you didn't really know personally, or they just weren't talked about. But now, it's common to have a neighbor, coworker, relative, church member, or even your pastor struggling with such issues.

Each one of us has been affected in some way by the decline of moral standards in our society, and Bob Reccord has stepped up to the plate to provide biblical insight and personal wisdom as he boldly addresses this painful subject, which affects so many men and women. As a businessman, pastor, and national Christian leader, Bob has witnessed how moral failure can shipwreck not only a marriage but a promising ministry as well. He has served as a counselor to fellow Christians and has helped to guide many people toward healing and restoration.

The lessons Bob has learned from these hurting people are valuable. And it's with a spirit of caring for fellow believers that he shares with readers. Bob doesn't deliver his message with finger wagging, but with a tone of compassion and solid, usable advice. His words are simple but profound.

Who needs this book? People who were tempted and failed to guard their heart? Sure, if you fit into that category, then you can certainly benefit. But, in my view, people who really need this book are those who least expect temptation to emerge from the still waters beneath, which can grab them without letting go and pull them under. Because, as Bob skillfully demonstrates, the dangers that lurk beneath are invisible, unexpected, and treacherous.

My friend, if you want to understand this devastating problem—because you lead and counsel others, because you're a caring mom, dad, or a young person wanting to head in the right direction, or because you're smart enough to know that you must guard your *own* heart— no matter what your stage in life is—then this book is for you.

John C. Maxwell
Founder, The INJOY Group

Introduction

The screeching sound could have awakened the dead.

Little did they know that within hours most of them would drown.

The jarring collision had thrown some to the floor, awakened others, and brought the celebrated party to a halt.

It couldn't be happening! They'd said it was impossible; this ship was unsinkable. How could something so secure, so trustworthy and stable, be in such desperate straits?

The source was a danger beneath the surface. A place where no one could see. The hidden recesses invisible to the common sight and power of observation. And equally to blame was an arrogant overconfidence that this great vessel was invincible and that nothing could alter its course.

And so it was on the night of April 14, 1912, that the *Titanic* sank to the bottom of the Atlantic in the frigid black of night, the victim of a giant iceberg hidden beneath the surface. While many later thought the

Titanic sank because of a massive hole punched into the upward hull, this was later disproved. Instead, the *Titanic* sank because of six narrow gashes running down the starboard side of the ship. The unsinkable luxury liner had lost a battle with its enemy below the waterline.

As the iceberg penetrated the brittle steel of the *Titanic*, water rushed into its supposedly watertight compartments, destroying the ship's buoyancy. It was later determined that the steel used to build the *Titanic* was of inferior quality, becoming brittle in the frigid waters of the North Atlantic.

And no one had seen the attack coming, because the ultimate danger was not above the waterline but below it.

That's true of icebergs. Formed by glaciers, then breaking off due to temperature changes, they float in the cold ocean waters. But the danger is that only one-seventh to one-ninth of the iceberg is ever visible above the surface. Most of the iceberg lays beneath the surface and is lethal for anyone who sails too near.

You already know the *Titanic*'s tragic toll—more than fifteen hundred dead, including millionaires John Jacob Astor, Benjamin Guggenheim, and Isadore Strauss. The time taken to sink—less than three hours. The lifeboats and life vests—totally inadequate. And the speed of the ship—much too fast and overconfident in dangerous waters.

And the real tragedy is that it could have been avoided. Warnings went unheeded. In fact, at least six warnings of ice fields were ignored. One was never delivered to the bridge. Another was ignored due to the *Titanic*'s wireless operator's carrying out his own agenda and not wanting to be interrupted. And the captain was drifting in and out of sleep in his cabin. If only someone had paid attention to the warnings and been on guard!

I find that too many marriages are like the *Titanic*. Struck by dangers lurking beneath the surface. Sinking quickly, killing those on board. Tragedies with victims. Avoidable tragedies caused by overly confident captains, fast-paced lifestyles, foolish priorities, unstable structures, dangers out of sight. Shipwrecks waiting to happen.

I hear about these sinking vessels all the time. And here's the scary part: In the Christian community, I find an increasing number of failing marriages to be among our leaders. The statistics hit me like cold water in the face because I care—and, frankly, because I'm in a position to be concerned.

As president of an organization spanning the North American continent with more than five thousand missionaries, twenty-five hundred chaplains, and literally millions of laypeople who have adopted an evangelistic lifestyle that we call being *on mission* for God, I hear about shipwrecked marriages every few days. Rarely does a week go by that I don't learn of another one. I receive telephone calls and E-mails and visits from people—usually dedicated Christians—who have hit an iceberg while they were foolishly traveling at high speeds, believing their marriage was shipshape when, in reality, it was vulnerable to sinking, and their whole family was at risk.

I both welcome and dread my encounters with these people because of the pain and hurt and fear I will experience along with them as they pour out their stories. But the amazing thing is that most stories contain several very common threads. Several points of vulnerability—like inferior steel and hidden icebergs—that shouldn't have been lethal, if only the people had been on guard.

In the interest of not only our homes and marriages but also the generations to come, I have collected several simple but powerful principles learned from the stories I too often hear. I am sharing these safeguards in this book, so that you too can be on guard.

I

Standing Tall or Falling Flat

I had a friend who was brilliant off the charts. He'd played college football and started on a winning Orange Bowl team. He was well liked by friends and successful in his work.

But one day his life fell apart.

Many nights he had surfed the Net, first looking up stock quotes and low prices for airfare and the latest sports scores, especially for his alma mater. Then he stumbled across a porn site. His jaw almost dropped. The images were riveting. Grinding bodies. Up close and *very* personal. All in living color. He heard his wife down the hall, so he clicked away and went back to the news. A few days later, while checking E-mail, he clicked again and again, looking for the site. *Where did it go?* He gave up and went to bed.

But the images swam in his mind during those drowsy minutes before sleep, and the next night he

5

looked again. This time he found it. A hyperlink took him to another site and then another. It was easy. And he wanted more.

Soon he found a chat room. He hung out there, mostly "listening," learning the protocol, the rules. The thing was, there were no rules. The protocol was to talk as dirty as possible. He wondered if he could. He waited and finally tried. This was easy too. No one knew him. In his suit and tie at work—certainly at church!—no one would believe he could type such vile things on his keyboard. But in a matter of minutes he could "experience" more—vicariously, of course—through his new-found friends in the chat room than he'd ever experienced in his wildest imagination. In fact, his imagination and his minutes in the chat room began to blend. Then one day, when a woman typed a message suggesting they meet, he wrote back yes.

But he didn't meet her. He never met her. *Lost my nerve,* he thought, when he was down on himself. *Got a grip,* he told himself, when he remembered his wife and kids and the words he said at the altar. *It was different with me. I could handle it.*

Seems my friend was a Christian. He "kept his grip" for a few more months, occasionally visiting the chat room, surfing the sites, then switching back to E-mail or sports scores when his wife or son or daughter came around. It was easy. Too easy.

He noticed his wife could be pretty grouchy some-times. But if she found him doing E-mail late at night, she kept quiet. "Too little time at the office," he said. She seemed willing to let it go.

The images and words and ideas seeped into his mind on the job. He became distracted, so occasionally he would interrupt his work projects for a quick surf to a porn site. A minute or two there was enough at first. He kept the desires at bay, especially when he was having a stressful day. But the raunchier the visit, the less satis-fied he felt. He wanted to "talk." He would click to a chat room, share real-time thoughts. One day a second "let's meet" message came across his screen. This time he did it.

He knew once would be enough when he left the motel. He would never return. It was disgusting, and he needed a good bath. *I need to have my head examined,* is what he thought.

It was weeks before he clicked on anything more rad-ical than the weather. But one day he fell. More hard-core porn. More chatty porn addicts. The second liaison led to an affair.

It was torrid. Well, she didn't exactly match the images on the screen, but she was certainly more enthu-siastic in bed than his wife of more than two decades. At least it seemed that way. *Maybe because when we get together sex is the agenda . . . no, no, no!* He chased that idea out of his head while driving into the garage. *It's because she really understands me.*

My friend is real. I love him, but I hate what he did. Not just to his wife and kids but to himself. And to all of us who believe in fidelity, revere God's Word, and honor our commitments. What he did brings all of us down. It affects not just him but us.

Because of him—and many others I know—our moral fabric is shredding. A culture of lust is overtaking our society. Lies are becoming easier to say . . . and believe.

The fallout is everywhere. Even if I didn't read the news, I could tell by the number of telephone calls I receive from people in distress, my increasing number of E-mails describing desperation, and the visits to my home and office from people with sad, sordid tales to tell.

In a few pages I will share the E-mail from his daughter. It was written from her to her father. She forwarded it to me to use in the book, for you to read. (An excerpt: "I cannot comprehend the sincerity of anything you say anymore, Dad . . . You say that you would die for me, but you were unwilling to live for me . . . I am learning that words are a cheap commodity, especially your words . . . I am angry with you for living a life of deception and for going against everything you have ever taught me to be true and right . . . I disrespect you as a man, as a husband, and as a father.") More on her E-mail later in what I think you'll find to be a short, easy-to-learn-from book. And one with answers for this problem of protecting our marriages from the damage of lust . . . answers for you and for me.

Oh, you may think: *This doesn't apply to me. I'm older and wiser. I'm happily married. I'm a Christian.* Hey, my friend would have said the same things. So would the other people I'll tell you about in this book. All fell victim to sexual compromise because they failed to apply some very simple principles.

For one thing, they lied to themselves. They rationalized and justified their thoughts and actions with ideas like these (my comebacks are in parentheses):

- I can handle this; I won't let it get out of hand. (Oh, really? Can you play with a baby cobra and not get bitten?)

- God wants me to be happy. (Hm-m, I thought His Owner's Manual said He wants you to be holy.)

- I don't want anybody to get hurt. (News flash! There's no such thing as a safe affair.)

- You just don't understand my situation. (Oh, sure, you're unique.)

I guess the cat's out of the bag; I don't agree with the lies.

Let's explore just the last one, flesh it out a bit with words I often hear. "You just don't understand my situation. It's different with me. If you had to deal with the spouse I have, you'd understand! You don't know the stress I'm under; I've just *got* to have relief. I don't feel the love anymore like I used to. This [new] person really understands me."

I hear these all the time, and I seem to be hearing them more. (The friend I described hit each one.)

As infidelity becomes more common, I see how easy it is to fall into the trap.

Temptation is everywhere. Recently I was between flights, so I stopped in the airport newsstand. Just wanting a little brain food, I headed for the magazine rack. Among titles of articles splashed across magazine covers on the general (not adult) market: "Pretzel Sex," "Sex with Strangers," "Better Sex through Gourmet Cooking," "Sex—from Good to Great—What's the Secret?" These titles were out in the open in a highly public place, not even hidden beneath the surface of wrappers. Think of the icebergs waiting to shipwreck your life whenever you stroll up to a magazine rack, log on to the Internet, or flip on the TV!

And the worst part is that people are succumbing—and so many of them are God's people. A few examples:

- A national ministry leader in a country outside the United States recently told me he estimates that at least 50 percent of the pastors in his country have toyed with Internet pornography.

- A woman responsible for placing missionaries confided in me that she sometimes must perform the very distasteful task of removing a missionary from the field because of moral failure. One who was discharged because of his addiction to Internet porn shocked her when he said he didn't see anything wrong with his habit "because it's a private activity and doesn't hurt anyone."

- A confidential survey was conducted among 350 men from a dozen evangelical denominations, according to Patrick A. Means in *Men's Secret Wars*.[1] Of these, 64 percent struggle with sexual addiction or sexual compulsion, including but not limited to using pornography, compulsive masturbation, or other secret sexual activity; 25 percent admit to having had sexual intercourse with someone other than their wife—since becoming a Christian; 14 percent acknowledge having had sexual contact short of intercourse outside of their marriage—since becoming a Christian.

- An executive at a huge communications conglomerate reported that, when his company was market testing a new television product via participating hotels, they discovered that the requests for porn programs went up exponentially when conventions of evangelicals were in town.

So, naturally, I'm concerned. I see not only the world sinking but also God's people—pastors, missionaries, chaplains, and leaders committed to spreading the gospel but who are too often attacked themselves by lethal dangers lurking beneath the surface.

I believe there's a way out of this disaster . . . and, best of all, there's a way to keep the trapdoor shut, a way to keep the marriage commitment watertight. First, some background.

1. Patrick A. Means, *Men's Secret Wars* (Grand Rapids: Revell, 1999), 132–33.

2

Honoring Sexual Fidelity or Laughing at It

My first boy-girl experience was humiliating but insightful. I was eight, and Cathy was nine. She played army with me and the other neighborhood kids on warm summer days. Our battlefields were backyards and alleys. Our sniper positions were trees.

On this day I was having a blast and figured she was too. But above the noise of my plastic gun going rat-tat-tat, I heard Cathy rallying the troops. She was changing the game! With the persuasive personality of a field marshal, she called a cease-fire and declared a new game.

Seems Cathy suddenly wanted to play wedding. And before I could get off another good round at our enemy hiding in the bushes, she had convinced the other soldiers to assume their positions in front of her imaginary altar as a wedding party. *How could they be so dumb?* I thought as I dropped to the ground from a sturdy oak branch.

Then I realized what a trap I was in. She wanted me to play the groom, and the other guys were going along with it!

"If Somebody Knew Me"

The heart of many women is revealed by Barbara Streisand in the movie *The Mirror Has Two Faces*. In one scene, Streisand talks with her friend, Doris, about marriage. Proclaiming her disdain, Doris questions, "What is marriage anyway? A ring, a contract, fighting and compromising . . ."

"No," responds Barbara. "It can be more than that. I'll tell you what I envy about people in love. I'd love it if somebody knew me—really knew me. What I like. What I'm afraid of. What kind of tooth-paste I use. I think that would be really wonderful!"

There it is. Do you see it? The woman's main yearning is not for a big income, a five-bedroom house in an affluent suburb, a Lexus or BMW in the garage, and charge cards from major stores. It's much simpler than that. It's to be known at the depths of who she is. It's to have interest expressed, even in the smallest things of life. It's to feel that what she likes and dislikes really matters to her man—and that he accepts her no matter what.

I was disgusted with the whole lot of 'em but finally rambled into the house to borrow one of Dad's ties. (What self-respecting eight-year-old boy would want a tie of his own?) With it twisted around my neck, I reluctantly took my place—by her side, of course. (Oh, didn't I mention that Cathy had cast herself as the bride?) As she positioned the minister and the best man and the bridesmaids, she said in her best someday-my-prince-will-come voice: "Someday I'll have a *real* wedding. My groom will love me and cherish me and fulfill all my dreams. We'll go on a wonderful honeymoon, and then we'll live happily ever after!"

Someone who will love me, cherish (or respect) me, and fulfill all my dreams. Now years later and, hopefully, a bit wiser, I've come to realize that's what every woman wants from adolescence through adulthood. And, frankly, that's eventually what every man wants too—a marriage relationship that brings out his best, not his worst, laying a foundation for the best that life can be. Let's take a closer look at this expectation.

Someone who will love me. This is easy to say but much more challenging to experience. The key in this phrase is *love,* a word that too often rolls off the tongue in flippant flattery or intentional manipulation. Love is a complex concept, yet we apply it to define our preferences about everything from a person to a color. But the Bible describes a kind of love that's meant to be found

"And That's When I Knew I Loved You"

I recall one of the greatest compliments my wife Cheryl ever gave me. She asked, "Did I ever tell you what ultimately made me fall in love with you?" I paused, then shook my head. Cheryl launched into a memory involving another student she'd been dating.

"Oh, he was a talented guy, but the longer we dated, the more I realized that he wanted me to celebrate his victories, yet he never seemed to celebrate mine. In fact, he seemed a bit threatened when I experienced them. But then one day at a campus meeting that I was leading, I looked over and saw you leaning against the wall, gazing at me—and you were smiling. That's when I realized you were as happy to see me succeed as you were to experience success yourself. And that's when I knew I loved you."

I will carry that compliment to my grave because it meant so much to me. It also reminds me of this reality: Every one of us wants and needs love and respect, because those qualities will help us survive the storms that time, inevitably, brings.

in all marriages to keep the relationship secure, healthy, and growing.

The Scripture most often used in weddings comes from 1 Corinthians 13. It describes the love that God intends for people to experience in relationships that are operating at their best, that are the most satisfying, that most closely resemble God's perfection. The precise word God chose for *love* in this Scripture is not a word that means brotherly love or erotic love. It's the kind of love with which God loves us. The Greek New Testament word is *agape*. It describes a love that gives and keeps on giving, regardless of the response.

"Love is patient, love is kind. It does not envy, it does not boast, it is not proud. It is not rude, it is not self-seeking, it is not easily angered, it keeps no record of wrongs. Love does not delight in evil but rejoices with the truth. It always protects, always trusts, always hopes, always perseveres. Love never fails" (1 Cor. 13:4–8).

Are you experiencing this kind of love in your marriage? Consider these questions:

- When you're on time but your spouse isn't, are you patient?

- When your spouse needs attention but you're focused on a task, are you understanding?

- When your spouse succeeds in his or her own sphere of strength, are you the enthusiastic cheerleader?

- Do you mention how much you've done in the past when you're trying to get the upper hand during a disagreement in the present?

- Do you ever use your spouse as the butt of your jokes or the target of your one-liners?

- Do you ever leave the impression with your mate that it's your way or the highway?

- When you're watching your favorite show or reading your favorite book but your mate wants to talk, are you willing to stop and listen?

- Do you keep short accounts or detailed records of hurts from the past?

- When your mate happens to be wrong, does your heart want to scream, "Gotcha! I knew I was right!"

- Are you willing to look for the best and overlook the worst?

- Are you willing to hang in there when the easier response would be to hang it up?

Your answers to questions like these can make all the difference in marriages that last compared with marriages that collapse. And remember, the key to a wonderful marriage is not simply to find a great mate . . . but, even more basic, to *be* a great mate.

Someone who will cherish or respect me. Every woman needs to feel cherished, and every man needs to be respected, and both are essential ingredients in marriages that succeed.

I'm careful about generalizations based on gender, but here's one I've found true in my own experience: Women generally communicate through sharing and feeling, and men interact on the levels of thinking and doing. I believe it's because women are more relational, and men are more action-oriented.

So what does it mean to be cherished? To a woman this means sharing deeply, feeling secure that she's well understood and accepted for who she is. She wants her husband to desire her *only*. She wants assurance that she's pleasing him completely. She wants to be known intimately by him.

Every man wants to be respected and admired by the woman in his life. He wants to know that she looks to him for protection and security and that she sees him as adequate in the important areas of life and relationship. In the deepest part of his heart, he needs her to make him feel significant.

Isn't it ironic that—when infidelity breaks the marriage vows—it also cuts the emotional cords that both the husband and the wife so desperately want and need? I think of a couple I know, Sam and Jennifer. When Sam had an affair, Jennifer experienced distrust and insecurity—and for good reason. She was sharing him, which is the opposite of being cherished. And Jennifer's respect and admiration for Sam diminished because of his weakness. They both lost what they wanted and needed most.

Someone who will help fulfill all my dreams. How in the world can this need ever be fulfilled? It may not be as difficult as it sounds. The seed of this dream in every person's heart is the desire to find someone who helps us fulfill all that we have the potential to be. It's the depth of our soul crying out to that significant person in our life, "Help me soar with my strengths . . . and help me manage my weaknesses."

All the men and women I've ever known desire with all their heart to reach the potential for which they were created, but they don't want to do it alone. They want to share the journey with someone special—someone who won't be threatened by their success but, instead, will realize that, as they help each other reach their ultimate potential, each will be far more fulfilled *together* than they ever would have been separately.

By the time I was a teenager, and girls had taken on a whole new significance in my life, I remembered my childhood friend Cathy's words about marriage. I came to the conclusion that her dreams weren't so bad. Those were the days of *Ozzie and Harriet, Father Knows Best,* and *Leave It to Beaver.* They were innocent times for me and my friends, only one of whom had divorced parents. The rest of us had his or her parents still living together, and the word *affair* wasn't even in our vocabulary.

Despite all the changes in our culture, God has hard-wired every woman, beginning when she was a little girl, to dream about a husband who would sweep her off her feet in love and cherish her for the rest of her life. The dream is that he would love and cherish her more than anything or anyone else.

As I matured into my late teen years, I found that God also structured every man to need a woman in his life. His dream is that she would respect and honor him and support his leadership in their home.

The dreams are there because God has placed His eternal design in the hearts of His creations. The Bible says, "He has set eternity in the hearts of men" (Eccles. 3:11). Two key relational principles in His eternal design are: (1) each of us would have a vertical relationship with Him that is personal and intimate; (2) the most personal and intimate horizontal relationship in the entire world would be between husband and wife. God put both desires in our hearts because He knew that was how we would ultimately be most fulfilled, and the quality of the horizontal always depends on the quality of the vertical.

It is God's plan that, in marriage, both the man and the woman would grow to fulfill their most strategic roles. Each person's role would find maximum enrichment through God's plan for both man and woman in the fulfillment of marriage.

The man's primary role is to provide leadership and direction to the home. He leads by being sure that he has a faithful relationship with God and a fruitful relationship with his wife. In his role as servant leader, he commits to loving his wife sacrificially with Christ as his model. Whatever is needed to create an atmosphere of love, honor, and maximum growth, he will do. The husband's role is far more a responsibility than it is a right or a privilege. As leader, he is responsible under God to provide for the needs of all those in his charge and care.

Complementing the husband is his soul mate, his wife. By God's eternal design, she is the helper who comes alongside and complements him in every area of his responsibility. She is also the child-bearer, as well as the child-nurturer. The context of this responsibility is the home where the wife is the manager of the day-in and day-out environment and activities.

God's intention is for a marriage to be full of joy, regularly growing and supremely fulfilling. That's always God's plan for us. In fact, it's the very reason He sent His Son—so that we might have a fully abundant life grounded in a vertical relationship with Him in order for our horizontal relationship with others to operate at their maximum potential. And at no greater place is that true than in the incredible gift of marriage.

Unfortunately, things have changed! Although God's truths are eternal, life in the twenty-first century is far different from life in my Leave-It-to-Beaver youth. Someone recently said to me that today young adults look around and see everyone getting married while middle-aged adults look around and see everyone getting divorced. A nationally known radio broadcaster recently commented that the new twenty-fifth anniversary gift is a divorce.

The marital bond is crumbling at its foundation. A key crack in the foundation is a sexually charged and saturated culture. Today sex attracts, tantalizes, entertains and sells—a tragic transition from the original purpose for which God created it within the boundaries of marriage. But like anything else taken out of its proper context and abused, what is meant as a gift can become the source of grief.

Many experts say that attitudes about adultery are shifting from outright condemnation to a rather uneasy acceptance. Estimates of married people engaged in extramarital affairs continue to soar while home after home crumbles. The soul of our society, as well as the future of the next generation, is at stake . . . and you and I hold in our hands the fragile future of our marriages and our homes.

The children and grandchildren of this generation are watching how we value marriage—whether our marriage covenants are honored or trashed. Is the marital relationship destined to be another victim of our disposable society? Is sexual fidelity a value to be honored or an outdated custom meriting only risqué humor? It's critical that we recapture the covenant of marriage and the centrality of sexual fidelity. We need to wake up and remember that the stumbling of one generation leads to the slippery slope of the next generation.

One researcher who studied eighty-six societies over the course of history has made an amazing discovery about sexual fidelity, calling it "the single most important predictor of a society's ascendancy. In human records, there is no instance of a society retaining its energy after a complete new generation has inherited the tradition that does not insist on prenuptial and post-nuptial continence."[1]

So at the beginning of this little book, for the sake of our society as well as for our homes and our children, I invite you to turn your heart back toward home. To do so you must intentionally place a guard at your heart's door. God knew we would struggle with this when He said, "Above all else, guard your heart, for it is the well-spring of life" (Prov. 4:23). He gives us the ability to accomplish this, but we must decide for ourselves that guarding our heart is necessary, and then we must resolve to do it.

1. Philip Yancey, *Finding God in Unexpected Places* (Nashville: Moorings, 1995), 16.

3

Setting Our Hearts on Evil or Setting Our Hearts on God

Where is that place we call the heart? We know the heart as the organ in our chest that pumps blood to the rest of our body. But is it something else? Did Hallmark invent the notion that our heart is a place where our emotions, attitudes, and sensibilities dwell? Hardly. I believe that's a biblical concept, and I'll show you why.

First, let's consider how the Bible's Old and New Testaments fit together. Some people who go to church seem to want to live in the Old Testament with its rules. Others prefer to camp out in the New Testament because of its emphasis on grace. The reality is that the Old and the New Testament are like a lock and a key, a hand and a glove. One is incomplete without the other. Together they record God's redemptive history of expressing His love to us and desiring us to experience an intimate, personal relationship with Him, vertically, so that we

Remembering Her Wild Period

It had been more than a decade since what Kathy called her wild period—six years of sexual abandon, four in college and two as a single woman living in the city. Somehow she'd managed to slip through those years without succumbing to a sexually transmitted disease or getting pregnant.

But tonight Kathy lay in bed beside her sleeping husband Brad, a loving man who provided well for her and the kids—and who came home to *her* every night. He was snoring gently, but she was wide awake. Images of other men kept popping into her head, despite the fact that Brad was a wonderful lover. Not only images but feelings. Feelings of guilt, shame, confusion—what she had suffered during the wild period when she sought total freedom.

And now these feelings were coming to the surface. They were crowding out the good feelings of joy and wholeness and security she should be feeling. During her wild period Kathy believed the lie that she would be able to put all this behind her when she settled down to become a faithful wife, as she eventually did. But the memories haunted her—like tonight, when love was supposed to be pure and beautiful and good.

She plumped her pillow. It would be a long night.

can maximize our relationships with one another, horizontally.

If you study the Bible, you'll find that the Old Testament has a wonderful series of illustrations, but it also includes principles of the New Testament. In fact, the apostle Paul says in 1 Corinthians 10:6, "Now these things occurred as examples to keep us from setting our hearts on evil things as they did." What "things" can Paul be talking about?

Paul refers to events of the Old Testament when the people acted on the motivations of their misguided hearts, usually with disastrous results. We are told that these stories are to be *examples* to us. But why? It's to keep us from making the same mistakes *with our hearts* that many in the Old Testament made.

Repeatedly in the Old Testament, God talks about the importance of the heart. He says it's the *center of everything that we are*. God told Samuel that while man looks on the outward appearance of things, God focuses on the heart (1 Sam. 16:7).

God's people adopted this verse to guide them. Even today, Jewish people hold this verse in reverence and refer to it as the Shema, and Jesus called it the greatest commandment:

> *Hear, O Israel:* The LORD our God, the LORD is one. Love the LORD, your God with all your heart and with all your soul and with all your strength. These commandments that I give you today are to be

upon your hearts. Impress them on your children. Talk about them when you sit at home and when you walk along the road, when you lie down and when you get up. Tie them as symbols on your hands and bind them on your foreheads. Write them on the doorframes of your houses and on your gates (Deut. 6:4–9).

"These commandments . . . are to be written upon your hearts . . . tie them as symbols on your hands . . . write them on the doorframes of your houses . . ." Clearly, God wanted His children to know Him deep within their very beings—that place we call the heart.

When Israel wandered away from God, they were said to have allowed their hearts to wander. Israel's history of wandering—both physically and spiritually— was recorded as an example for us so we would not make the same mistake with our hearts. Obviously, God wants us to set our hearts on Him, not on evil.

I have found that often when God has given us examples of what to emulate and what to avoid, they are set forth so we can compare and contrast them. The stories of Joseph and David are like that. Let's compare and contrast these two men who grappled with one of the greatest temptations of life—sex. One kept his heart focused on God, and the other allowed his heart to drift toward evil. One man stood firm, and the other man fell flat.

In Genesis 39 we find the intriguing story of Joseph, who had been sold into slavery as a result of his own brothers' jealousy. After being transported to Egypt, he was sold to the head of Pharoah's secret service. The Bible makes clear that God blessed Joseph, and because he was blessed, others around him experienced good things too. Isn't that just like God? When He blesses any of us, the blessings spill over to those around us.

But all these blessings didn't go unnoticed. The Bible says Joseph was well built and handsome, and Potiphar's wife set her eyes on this young hunk. Perhaps she was bored because Potiphar was a workaholic and gone a lot. Maybe she felt Potiphar was more in love with his work than with her. Regardless of the motivation, she put the moves on Joseph, asking him to go to bed with her . . . and Joseph was faced with a decision. Fortunately, he made the right choice.

Later in the Bible another man is given to us as an example. Faced with a similar opportunity to make a life-determining choice, he—unfortunately—made the wrong one.

In 2 Samuel 11, King David strolled across the palace roof at night. Looking over the city he ruled as king, his eyes fell on a captivating yet dangerous sight. A beautiful woman was luxuriating in a bath under the moonlit sky.

Like Joseph, David was confronted head-on with a decision. The choice he would make would affect not only the moment but also his legacy. What would he do? Unfortunately, David took the wrong turn.

Temptation Lurks

I can identify with Joseph. Seems that no matter how welll think my life is going or how solid is my commitment as a Christian and a husband, temptation lurks around the most unexpected corners.

After speaking in Dallas, I went back to my hotel room late one evening just to kick back. I flipped on the TV and began surfing. I avoided certain channels because I've learned their danger, but I did land on HBO. It took me a few moments to figure out what the program was. Suddenly, it dawned on me that there, on a major network, was a special on exotic dancers—with nothing left to the imagination.

My heart told me to flip the channel—now! But another voice inside said, "Stay . . . just for a while. You'll enjoy this . . . it'll only get better!"

Like Joseph, I was faced with a decision that only I could make. Thankfully, long ago I had decided what my course of action would be when faced with such enticements. So the channel was changed—and quickly! But not without tempting second thoughts.

Some of us are shocked when temptations and potentially tragic choices come knocking on our door. But all of us are vulnerable because we're part of a fallen world, and we must question whether spiritual pride and arrogance are blinding us to that fact.

"The Choices I Made"

David's wrong turn was similar to the tragic choices made by a friend of mine who tumbled into an adulterous affair.

As he fought to put his life and marriage back together, he E-mailed to me these sobering words: "Last year I did things I never thought I was capable of doing. When I look back and think, it almost seems like this is something that happened to someone else, but it wasn't. It happened to me because of the choices I made. If I were someone else who had been a witness to my life and actions last year, I would be shaking my head in disbelief as to how a person could come to behave in that way and for such an extended period of time. I have no excuse; I have no one to blame; there was no injustice in my life; and I am responsible for the decisions that were made and the actions that occurred."

Interspersed among modern examples throughout this book will be a closer look at the lives of Joseph and David. Walk with me through the decisions they made and the principles that undergirded their actions.

4

Recognizing Our Weaknesses or Overestimating Our Strengths

After a meeting in Washington, D.C., I ran into my friend, Dr. Joe Stowell, president of Moody Bible Institute. Toward the end of our conversation, I asked Joe, "Share with me the greatest challenge you're facing in the days ahead, so I can pray for you." Without hesitation, but with a mischievous grin, Joe responded, "My biggest challenge is the same as yours, Bob. My biggest challenge is *me!*"

Joe nailed it. He nailed it for Joe, he nailed it for me, and he nailed it for you! To quote Pogo from the comic strip, "We have met the enemy, and the enemy is us!"

The crux of Joe's declaration is that each of us is the product of our own choices. We not only make them, but we're responsible for them. The ones we make determine what—and who—we become. And when we make poor ones, the consequences just keep on coming.

When each of us comes to know God in a personal relationship through Christ, God powers our inner being with an alarm system. It's set to sound a warning when we're in danger of crossing over the well-intentioned boundaries He has established for our lives. Without this warning we tend to overestimate our strengths. We think we can control our impulses on our own. Recovering alcoholics know they have no business in a bar. Sure, they could order a cup of coffee and have a great chat with the friendly bartender. But, sooner or later, after that barrier comes down, another will follow. *I could stop after one little drink,* they might think. The wise alcoholic, who's in a good recovery program and depends on God, knows his own weakness and doesn't take that first step—into the bar.

These boundaries can readily be found in God's Owner's Manual—the Bible.

I was reminded of this truth not long ago when I was waiting to get my car serviced. It's amazing what you'll read when you're bored. Picking up an automotive magazine, I came across an interesting question-and-answer column asking, "What's the most unread book in America?" Being in the ministry, my mind raced to a typical answer—the Bible. I was dumbfounded when I read this magazine's answer—the car owner's manual. I almost laughed out loud.

The more I thought about it, the more sense it made. The car owner's manual is written to ensure that the vehicle operates at maximum effectiveness and avoids major breakdowns. But few people seem to have read their car owner's manual—until. Until their vehicle isn't operating at maximum effectiveness or has experienced a major breakdown.

We're a lot like that with God's Owner's Manual. He's written it out of His deep and abiding love for us to ensure that we operate our lives at maximum effectiveness, and He provides us with a written preventive maintenance plan to avoid major breakdowns. But like car owners we often wait too late to know what we need to know.

His Owner's Manual warns that an inevitability of life will be temptation and for a simple reason: As humans we have a sinful nature at the very center of our being. Many people think the word *sin* describes our actions or attitudes. Actually, these are *evidences* of our sinful nature because sin is not so much *what* we do as *who* we are. Without a personal relationship with God through Christ, we are separated from Him and desperately in need of transformation from the inside out. Our inner sinful nature is determined to live life *our* way and do things *our* way rather than God's way—according to the Owner's Manual.

Different personality types express this sinful nature in different ways. Some people express it in active and

"I Decided to Disconnect the Wires"

I can remember waiting on the phone as I listened to the ringing at the other end of the line. I dreaded the moment Stan would answer.

Stan had been a friend for years. We'd spoken together on national programs, traveled together, had coffee and meals together, laughed together, prayed together, and shared openly about life together ... or so I thought. I'd just learned that he was discovered in an ongoing affair. His wife walked away. And, being a minister, Stan was relieved of his position.

When finally I heard a voice at the other end, all I could do was blurt out: "How could you do it? Didn't you realize what was happening? Weren't there alarms going off, at least when the affair was in danger of beginning?"

His response reminded me of the hush at a funeral home when someone has died. After what seemed to be an interminable, deafening silence, he hesitantly responded, "Yes, Bob. There were warnings. I heard the alarms of my conscience and God's Word clanging within my life ... but I decided to disconnect the wires."

observable rebellion. They lie to themselves about their own strengths, claiming, "I have the ability to stop this behavior at any time." Others cloak it in passive indifference, ignoring their weaknesses.

Even secular authorities have found the danger of this inner nature. Several years ago, the Minnesota Crime Commission did a study concerning the exponential rise of crime. What was driving it? Where was the root cause to be found? This spiritually neutral body came to a most interesting conclusion: "Every baby starts life as a little savage. He is completely selfish and self-centered. He wants what he wants when he wants it—his bottle, his mother's attention, his playmate's toy, his uncle's watch. Deny these, and he seethes with rage and aggressiveness, which would be murderous, were he not so helpless. He is, in fact, dirty. He has no morals, no knowledge, no skills. This means that all children, not just certain children, are born delinquent. If permitted to continue in the self-centered world of his infancy, given free reign to his impulsive actions, to satisfy his wants, every child would grow up a criminal, a thief, a killer, a rapist."

Amazingly in harmony with the Bible, don't you think? Even the secular experts recognize the reality of our nature!

Our sinful nature is ripe and ready when temptation comes along if we haven't experienced the transforming grace of God through Christ. God's Word tells us there are ways that seem right in our own eyes, but the destination of those ways is death and destruction because they're not God's ways (Prov. 16:25). And the Bible makes clear that temptation *will* come. James 1:13 says: "When tempted, no one should say, 'God is tempting me.' For God cannot be tempted by evil, nor does he tempt anyone." Notice it doesn't say "if." Instead, it says "when" we are tempted.

Joseph's *when* happened in the middle of work— unexpectedly—like a chance meeting at the proverbial water fountain or a cubicle conversation that becomes inappropriately personal or a business lunch that stirs longings for more than the agenda. As he carried out his job, Joseph found himself face to face with the possibility of violating the deepest point of his integrity—his truthfulness to himself, his employer, and his God.

David, on the other hand, was confronted with his *when* while taking a casual stroll. In a moment of leisure, he found himself drawn into a trap—like an outing at the beach when the opposite sex walks by with little left to the imagination or sitting at a computer when surfing a porn site seems like a harmless diversion or chatting at a party when things at home haven't been going so well and a neighbor of the opposite sex becomes all too willing to listen and console. David overestimated his strength to resist and ignored his weaknesses.

What amazes me about temptation is that Satan has never changed his predominant method. It's written clearly in the story of Adam and Eve. When Satan tempted Eve, he took her through a three-step process.

1. He questioned God by saying, "Did God say. . . ?"
2. He contradicted God by saying that God really didn't mean what He had said.
3. He replaced God. Satan made Eve believe she could depend on herself instead of God.

Satan has not changed his tactics at all. When tempting any of us, he still raises the question, "Did God really say (fill in the blank)?" Once he has gotten us to question whether God really gave us boundaries and guidelines for our benefit, then he contradicts God. He assures us that God didn't mean (fill in the blank). And when he gets us to the point of buying his contradiction of God's Word, he replaces God with us! Then we become our own God, and we do away with all absolutes. Whatever we desire to do, that becomes absolute. Whatever we say is true, that becomes true, and absolute truth suddenly becomes a moving target with no stability and no solid foundation. And the tragic result is that everything in life becomes relative.

Things become relative in our lives because we adopt wrong thinking. Wrong thinking about God. Wrong thinking about God's guidelines. Wrong thinking about what will satisfy. We may embrace thoughts like these:

- God doesn't have my best interest at heart.
- God is all about rules, and what I want is relationships.
- Nobody knows what I need like me.

When Satan's three-step process of temptation is combined with our wrong thinking, we can experience a failure to guard our heart. God has warned us that the heart of the problem in our lives is a problem of our heart. The Owner's Manual states, "The heart is deceitful above all things" (Jer. 17:9a).

Our deceitful heart leads to a process that can result in death. Deceit baits us and lures us into a trap like an unsuspecting animal. "Each one is tempted when, by his own evil desire, he is dragged away and enticed. Then, after desire has conceived, it gives birth to sin; and sin, when it is full-grown, gives birth to death" (James 1:14–15).

A part of us dies when we sin against God's loving parameters. Our conscience can die, our sensitivities can die, our gentleness and understanding can die, our willingness to ask forgiveness and make amends can die, and our relationships can die. And ultimately our receptivity to God dies.

But like every Owner's Manual, we are given instructions on how to avoid this disaster. The apostle Paul brings good news when he says, "No temptation has seized you except what is common to man. And God is faithful; he will not let you be tempted beyond what you

Deidre's Story

Listen to Diedre: "I still can't believe it happened. Basically, I had a good marriage. Two great kids. My youngest had just graduated. My husband Jason was doing great. He was given special responsibilities at work—and I was proud of him for that—but sometimes it made me feel he was married more to the job than to me, and I was in the background. With the kids gone, I was at loose ends.

"I don't know when Darren came into the picture. But suddenly I was aware of his presence in my life. He was interested in every detail about me, and when I entered the room, his face lit up like a sign, welcoming me into his world. It was exhilarating. Jason hadn't responded to me like that in years.

"I'd been taught that adultery is wrong, but I rationalized: *Doesn't God want me to be happy? Doesn't He want my intimacy needs fulfilled? Maybe He's even providing someone to fill the void.* And even worse: *God loves me and will overlook my wrongdoing.*

"Now I see how my temptation, rationalization, and action were just like Eve. I desired, I rationalized, and I took a bite. And to this day I'm still paying for that bite! How I wish I could undo the problems I've caused!"

can bear. But when you are tempted, he will also provide a way out so that you can stand up under it" (1 Cor. 10:13).

Isn't that just like God? Knowing that you and I would face tough times and the inevitability of temptation, He already provided an escape. And the escape is Jesus Christ, the Living Word of God, made known through the Scripture, the written Word of God.

Have you read recently how Christ Himself faced temptation after His baptism? If not, I would encourage you to get an easy-to-read, modern translation of the Bible, and turn to Matthew 3 and 4. Jesus met every temptation by knowing what the Owner's Manual said and following it step-by-step. I predict that if Jesus found it to be a good strategy for temptation, so will you and I.

As I travel across North America, I find a lot of church members claiming to be "a people of the Book." Unfortunately, when I talk to them about how much of the Bible they've internalized in their lives, I find that too often the results are dismal. It seems that many have gotten into the Book, but the Book hasn't gotten into them. Psalm 119:11 says, "I have hidden your word in my heart that I might not sin against you." I find in my own life that when I've made the effort to hide God's Word there, the likelihood decreases that I will sin and break God's heart and the heart of those around me.

If you're going to turn your heart toward home, it's crucial to pay attention to the Owner's Manual, so you can live at maximum effectiveness and avoid major breakdowns. For your sake—and for the sake of your children and grandchildren—remember it is only God who is able to keep you from falling (Jude 24–25).

5

Leaving Ourselves Wide Open or Guarding Our Hearts

Two men.

One stood tall.

The other fell flat.

Why? The answer to that question helps us to understand ourselves and learn from God's examples.

When you take time to study Joseph's life, one thing becomes clear. *Joseph understood his own weaknesses.* And that's because he knew himself well. He was realistic, and that's the first line of defense against leaving ourselves wide open.

That's not always easy to do in our culture. Identities are fragmented for so many reasons. Broken families. Abuse. Low morals splashed across the television and movie screen. The dark side of the Internet. A disposable society. A nation of victims.

But that's our world. Add to that a healthy dash of the secular, humanistic point of view that places man in the center of the universe as the source of everything, rather than God. Add two pinches of self-sufficiency. Mix in some superficiality. Stir with trials, disappointments, and heartache, and—*voila!*—you end up with a culture of people who don't have a realistic view of themselves. And—sensing this—they cover their weaknesses with a mask of strength bordering on arrogance.

How different Joseph was. He looked into the depths of his heart and recognized a problem, the first step toward guarding your heart.

Joseph could have identified with a New Testament personality, Paul. When Paul looked deeply into the recesses of his heart, he was honest enough to admit what he found: "I know I am rotten through and through so far as my old sinful nature is concerned. No matter which way I turn, I can't make myself do right. I want to, but I can't. When I want to do good, I don't. And when I try not to do wrong, I do it anyway" (Rom. 7:18–19 NLT).

That takes guts! While a lot of us spend our time trying to earn more money than we can imagine—to buy things we don't need, to impress people we don't even know—Joseph and Paul were getting in touch with who they really were.

Fleeing Temptation

A friend who knew his own weakness shared with me how he ran from pornography. Having once been attracted, he had made a commitment twenty-five years ago to run from it at every turn. He described an incident in a recent E-mail:

When I arrived at the Nashville airport, I found a new issue of *Penthouse* magazine in the bathroom stall, still in its sack from the store. Of course, I didn't seek its owner, although I expect he was pretty upset by his loss!

I hadn't looked at a pornographic magazine for more than twenty-five years, but I was still sorely tempted to take it to my hotel room and enjoy it. I could have done so easily and never been exposed by anyone. But I thought about my commitment to my life and, even more so, to my Lord. As I dropped the magazine into the bottom of a trash can, where no one would find it, I was still tempted to reach in and grab it, but immediately I felt a great sense of relief and accomplishment as I ran from the bathroom.

Self-awareness takes the courage to ask ourselves the right questions. For example:

- What things would I do if I felt that I would never get caught?
- Regardless of how important I say God is, how much time do I spend getting to know what He's like?
- How often do I find myself acting gracious on the outside but grating with anger on the inside?
- Who's in my life that I've chosen not to forgive because of wrong done to me?
- What are the three most important priorities in my life?
- How often is my mouth in motion before my mind is in gear?

The Owner's Manual can help us look deep inside, if we are brave enough to take the risk. God's desire is for us to be truthful enough to face our life as it *really* is rather than how we paint it to be. In Psalm 51:6, God says that more than anything else He wants us to experience truthfulness in our deepest parts. (That's the only way we can realize how desperately we need Him!)

We know Joseph had confronted the truth about his own weakness by his reaction to Potiphar's wife. He fled! He understood that he was not strong enough to handle the temptation. If he stayed, he would fall. It takes real strength to admit—and act on—a weakness.

An Interruption or a Contributor?

I recall early in my own marriage when I was ruthlessly task-oriented. My job was going well. My organization had experienced growth, and I was right in the middle of it. I was traveling thirty-three weeks a year while Cheryl was home with a four-year-old and a new baby. To this day, I shiver inside when I remember walking in from a trip, setting down my luggage and greeting Cheryl with, "Hi!" I could hardly wait to share with her all my successes. That's when I noticed she was crying.

She brought my world to a shattering halt. The sobering words she uttered are ingrained in my memory bank: "You know, you're getting to be more of an interruption to this family than you are a contributor to this family. Something's got to change. If it doesn't, I'm not sure where the kids and I will be a year from now."

She broke down and walked away. And I stood there, shell-shocked. What had I allowed to happen?

David overestimated his strengths. He was convinced that he could handle anything. After all, he was king! It's amazing how position, prominence, possessions, and privilege can fill us with such pride that we fail to see the fault lines in our character.

You and I operate in a hectic world. Cell phones and palm devices are electronic leashes. E-mail has made communications so rapid that we're exhausted just trying to keep up. In the sixteenth century, thousands of books were printed every year. Today, more than that are printed every day. The Boomer generation finds itself caught between adolescent children and aging parents. Sounds familiar, doesn't it?

I can identify with a statement made by Bill Hybels, the pastor of Willow Creek Community Church, Barrington, Illinois. Talking about the pressures of leadership, he became vulnerable enough with us to share that in the late 1980s he came face to face with fractures in his ministry and his marriage. His problems did not involve immorality, just enormous stress. My heart resonated when he said, "There came a time when the work of the church around me began to kill the work of God within me." I wonder if the work of being king around David began to kill the work of God within David. How about you? Can you relate?

Maybe you understand. You've been there. Or you're there now. While you're busy conquering your world, be careful not to be the one who ends up being conquered.

Besides busy people, God also faces challenges with gifted people—those who have so much to offer, who are talented beyond the norm, who—if they aren't careful—

can begin to rely more on their giftedness than on the God who granted the gift.

It was 1987, and I was invited to a Young Leaders Conference on the other side of the world. One of the leading names in evangelical Christianity was scheduled to be on the program. When I saw who was to speak, I was elated because I so respected his writings as well as his work.

I arrived at the auditorium early to get a good seat. I can't tell you the shock that ran through my heart when the master of ceremonies stood soberly before us and read a fax. The speaker had cancelled. He said he had looked so forward to being with us, but, unfortunately, he couldn't. He had committed moral failure. Rather than be with us, he must now stay home and begin to rebuild broken bridges. He asked for our forgiveness and our prayers. But then he warned each of us to guard our hearts, for out of it would come the issues of our lives. If we didn't guard it, he cautioned, we might one day find ourselves in shoes just like his.

Thankfully, through these years, I've seen this man go through a period of brokenness and redemption, but he's been restored to a very meaningful ministry. In addition he's become a great friend who constantly cautions me about relying more on the gift than on God and being so busy doing things *for* God that I miss the God for whom I claim to be doing the things.

Alert

What a warning for you and for me. It is not enough simply to guard what we believe to be the vulnerabilities of our lives—we must equally guard the strong points! Now, that's wisdom.

One further amazing insight from my friend. And it's grounded in the reality of experience. A few years ago, he shared with me, "Bob, all my life, people shared with me that Satan attacks at your weak points. And I believe that . . . and still do. But they didn't tell me the whole story. They didn't tell me that he equally attacks what you think are your strong points. For years, I said that if there was one place I would never have trouble, it was my marriage. I was committed to my wife and my family. I was intent on living a lifestyle that would please God. And I believe with all my heart that was an invulnerable strength. But that is the very place the adversary attacked so fiercely."

When I look at Joseph, who stood tall, and David, who fell flat, I come to one conclusion:

At any given moment, every one of us is only one step away from stupid.

6

Abusing Authority or Using Authority

Leadership is a privilege. With it comes many more responsibilities than rights. But, too often, we get these inverted.

John Maxwell shared with me a life-changing principle shortly after I came to know him. He compared leadership to a triangle with a broad horizontal axis at the base and a tall vertical axis through the center. Along the base, he wrote the word *freedom*, and along the vertical axis, he wrote the word *responsibility*. John explained that, when you don't have much responsibility, you've got lots of freedom. However, as your responsibility increases, your freedom decreases. The higher you go in leadership, the more you have to watch your actions and attitudes because of the ripple effect they have on everything and everyone around you. What a concept! It captures the whole issue of how we use our leadership positions. And each one of us has some role that either can be used faithfully or abused tragically: A parent . . . a coach . . . a ministry leader . . . a work supervisor . . . a confidant.

Joseph used his position responsibly and would do anything to avoid abusing it. When Potiphar's wife tempted him to go to bed with her, did you notice his response: "No one is greater in this house than I am. My master has withheld nothing from me except you, because you are his wife. How then could I do such a wicked thing and sin against God?" (Gen. 39:9).

Joseph understood that the key to handling leadership responsibly was accountability. He acknowledged explicitly his ultimate accountability to God and implicitly his accountability to Potiphar, his boss. Too many of us, especially in church life, feel that we're accountable to no one, covering it by saying, "I'm accountable to God alone." Tragically, I've found through the years that when leaders adopt this attitude it's only a matter of time until disaster strikes.

One practical aspect of accountability is that you must give someone the right to hold you to your promises—he or she won't *voluntarily* hold you accountable. To whom have you given the right to ask you the tough questions about life? I've found it tremendously helpful to select a few people to ask me probing questions that keep me accountable to the core of life's issues. Here are some samples:

- Have you seen anything on the Internet that you know you wouldn't watch if Christ were in the room with you?
- Have you had a desire for anyone other than your spouse?
- What are you doing to keep your body fit and rested?
- Are you spending both quality and quantity time with your spouse (and with your kids if they're still at home)?
- Are you giving a tenth of your income to the Lord?

And here's a question I learned from Chuck Swindoll a few years ago:

- Have you lied to me about any of the previous answers?

Years ago, while teaching at Dallas Theological Seminary with Leighton Ford and Dr. Howard Hendricks, Dr. Hendricks told me about a study he had done of over two hundred men in ministry who had fallen morally. Dr. Hendricks explained that he found a great deal of variation in their gifts, personalities, temperaments, and styles. But he found one commonality in every man: *They were accountable to no one.*

This is exactly where David found himself. As king, I'm sure he would have said he was accountable to God. Unfortunately, there was no one else in his life who held him accountable—not until Nathan confronted him in 2 Samuel 12. And then it was far too late!

David reminds me of another king in the Old Testament—Uzziah. His story is told in 2 Chronicles 26. An earlier chapter records his early days of being king,

---

A Double Life

A friend who cratered morally described it to me: "Somewhere in the process, I literally became two different people, living two separate, distinct lives. I made a series of bad choices, followed by sinful actions that ultimately led to a lifestyle—a double life—which horribly deviated from the standards set by God.

"Still, in order to rationalize and justify my behavior, I put up a wall and emotionally detached myself from real life. I was so fatigued and under so much stress that I only had energy to think about myself. Rather than caring for my family and serving them, I cared only for me, and I allowed myself to believe I was the one who was somehow being neglected."

He was gifted, busy—but not accountable—and that makes all the difference.

when he sought God regularly and feared God, understanding he was accountable to Him. In fact, the Scripture says, "As long as he sought the LORD, God gave him success" (v. 5).

But with success and position, sometimes there comes a deadening pride. The Scripture goes on to say: "His fame spread far and wide, for he was greatly helped [by the Lord] until he became powerful. But after Uzziah became powerful, his pride led to his downfall" (2 Chron. 26:15–16).

If you finish the story, you'll find that, when the priests tried to hold him accountable, he rebelled, telling them they had no right. After all, he was king! What a dangerous attitude—full of ourselves, empty of God, available to everyone, accountable to no one.

When was the last time you heard about a teacher abusing his or her authority and ending up in a sexual affair with a student? Or a coach with a player? Or a pastor with a parishioner? Or a boss with an employee? Or a president with an intern? None of us is invincible, and it would be great if we remembered it.

7

Making Disastrous Choices or Righteous Choices

After years of being a son, a student, a father, a businessman, a minister—and, especially, a husband, do you know what I find to be the greatest challenge of life? Choices! They make us or break us. And all of us have to make them.

We can ignore them. We can run from them. We can deny them. Or we can blame someone else for them, calling ourselves victims—a popular notion today.

But the only honest thing we can do is stand up and take responsibility for them.

I've heard so many excuses from those who've made poor moral choices. Confronted with temptation, they *chose not to avoid it*. They failed to understand that playing with immorality is like playing with a baby cobra. While it may be fascinating to look at, it's deadly to play with.

That's why God's Owner's Manual repeatedly warns us that when we face sexual temptation, there's only one correct choice to make—*run!* "Flee from sexual immorality. All other sins a man commits are outside his body, but he who sins sexually sins against his own body" (1 Cor. 6:18).

Listen again as the Bible says: "It is God's will that you should be sanctified: that you should avoid sexual immorality; and that each of you should learn to control his own body in a way that is holy and honorable, not in passionate lust like the heathen, who do not know God" (1 Thess. 4:3–5).

Notice that God leaves no question about the response He expects when the siren call of sexual temptation comes our way. God understands our inner nature enough to know that if we hesitate and float with the temptation, it's not a matter of *if* we will fall and fail, but only *when.*

Fleeing—that's exactly what Joseph did. He literally ran as hard as he could from the seductive invitation of Potiphar's wife.

The Bible doesn't tell us Joseph's thoughts, but here's one scenario of what might have raced through his mind: *With her help, I could literally sleep my way to the top. No one will ever know because I'm sure she won't tell. I have every right to do this because Potiphar isn't paying enough attention to her. What could this one time hurt? And I'm not really getting all I deserve for this job.*

It's true that Joseph was a man, and we know how many men think. But Joseph had guarded his heart. He was prepared to make the right choice instead of a disastrous choice. He *expected* temptation, and in preparation he had given control of his life to the Lord.

As a result, God protected Joseph in this situation, even *before* the woman tried to seduce him. Joseph

Small Choices—Big Results

My friend who had been addicted to pornography understands that small choices add up to big results. When he found a discarded issue of *Penthouse* in an airport bathroom, he immediately threw it away. He could have taken it to his hotel room. Who would have known?

The point is *he* would have known. And *God* would have known. He would have given in to a temptation that he knew was greater than he could resist. He made the right choice rather than a disastrous one.

Joseph made the same kind of choice. When the heat turned up, he cooled the circumstances by fleeing.

realized that he had nothing to gain—and everything to lose—by sleeping with Potiphar's wife: Her husband had given Joseph plenty of responsibility. (He was already at the top!) Joseph had the good sense to figure out that she was not discreet, because God had given him discernment. Joseph knew he had no right to sin against either God or his boss, not even one time. When she said,

---

Too Tired?

Maybe David was just plain tired. I recently read reports of the bragging battle going on among CEOs in North America. It seems they're competing with one another about how little they can sleep and still get the job done. They pride themselves on being able to work long hours and sleep short ones. It reminds me of college fraternity guys trying to see who can outdo the other. And it's not limited to men, as more and more women enter this elite group at the top of the business world.

The fact remains: Medical science has proven that the chemical balance for maximum effectiveness of our body requires seven to eight hours of sleep every night—whether you are a CEO or not.

And all of us know that when we're tired, our defenses fall.

"Come to bed with me!" Joseph refused and replied, "With me in charge, . . . my master does not concern himself with anything in the house; everything he owns he has entrusted to my care. No one is greater in this house than I am. My master has withheld nothing from me except you, because you are his wife. How then could I do such a wicked thing and sin against God?" (Gen. 39:7–9).

Joseph had made up his mind to flee *before* the temptation ever occurred. The question is, Have you? Will you make a disastrous choice or the right choice? I've found that the moment of temptation is no time to make choices of character because the heat of the moment melts our resistance.

Unfortunately, David made a disastrous choice. When the opportunity came, he was open to the possibility. Why? I don't know. After all, God had shown His hand powerfully at work in David's life for many years. He had led David, protected David, blessed David, honored David, and invited David into a personal relationship with Him. All that, and David still blew it. It reminds me that if David blew it, so could I . . . and so could you!

Perhaps, David, like many of us today, was stressed out. Understandably, the weight of responsibility of running a kingdom of people had to be more than just a little challenging. Constant complaints, major decisions, sandpaper people. Great successes, only to be followed by frustrating defeats.

Or perhaps David had allowed his priorities to shift from his life's work: 2 Samuel 11 begins with the words,

---

"Entry-Level Temptations"

David reminds me of a very good friend who suffered the same fate. My friend had been a man of faith who once cared for his kingdom: his job and his family. Still, he found his heart adrift.

And when the temptations came knocking . . . well, just listen to his words: "It was my inability to resist the 'entry-level' temptations that led to last year's events. It's pointless to ask me the question, 'What were you thinking?' Because the fact is, I simply wasn't thinking at all about what I was doing. I blinded myself to who and what I really was. My own selfishness prevented me from being loving as a husband should love his wife. And from that point, I began to detach myself emotionally from my marriage and my children. After I placed myself in this position, I was then open to the possibility of forming an emotional bond with another person."

"In the spring, at the time when kings go off to war . . ." David should have been someplace else—with his troops.

Maybe his wife had said something like, "You're gone so much in your work! Can't you stay home just a little while?" The tragic part is that even though David was "at home" physically, his heart was absent emotionally. Have you ever noticed that? In the hustle and bustle of today, amid the stress and strain, the busy schedules and the demanding deadlines, you can be at home without really being *at home*.

Perhaps that day as his wife had tried to talk to him, his eyes glazed over when he should have been listening. Perhaps his children needed his attention, but his response was, "Maybe another time." Or maybe things were tense at home, and he was rewarding himself with a lingering fantasy-filled life. It seems that his careless abandonment of responsibility caused him to be distracted and to drift emotionally, morally, and physically. It's no wonder that, when David saw a nude woman bathing, he was open to "entry-level temptation."

And so it was with David, and so it can be with us—unless we make the predetermined decision to run!

What is our response when major sin enters our lives—especially sexual sin? The answer is simple. We justify and rationalize. We look for ways to cover up what we've done so that we don't have to uncover *who* we are. We justify, and we rationalize. We lie not only to others but to ourselves. And so our problems increase, becoming deeper and more complex.

And it all begins with that first disastrous choice. Will you be like David? Or like Joseph, who made the righteous choice?

8

Justifying Our Actions or Facing Reality

I will share with you the four justifications and rationalizations I've heard most often through years of helping people grapple with this type of tragedy in their lives.

Rationalization #1
"I Can Handle This"

It's never ceased to amaze me how we can become so arrogant as to think, *I can handle this, and I won't let it get out of hand.* If you believe you can handle temptation and not let things get out of hand, ask yourself these questions:

- Are you ready for the fact that your spouse won't be able to invest his or her trust in you again for a very long time? You'll have to go to immeasurable

lengths to rebuild that trust, and—even then—
you'll never be sure that it's 100 percent returned.
A cloud of distrust will follow you wherever you
go, for as long as you go.

- Are you ready to sit down and explain to your
  children why you did what you did and watch the
  shock, hurt, disbelief, anger, and hopelessness in
  their eyes and faces?
- Are you ready for the very real threat of sexually
  transmitted diseases? With AIDS being at epi-
  demic proportions today—a disease for which
  there is no cure—are you willing to risk your life
  (and your spouse's life) for a few moments of
  pleasure?
- Are you ready for the emotionally ragged edges
  that will be left in your life if your spouse leaves
  you? How will you handle the ruptured
  relationship that will leave so much damage and
  hurt that regardless of how you look on the
  outside, a part of you will always be dying on
  the inside?
- What will you say to your parents? Are you ready
  to sit down and face them eye to eye and share
  with them honestly about such a stupid decision?
  What would it take to ever rebuild a relationship
  with them?
- Are you ready to surrender the respect of your
  colleagues, friends, and family members?
- If you're in ministry, are you ready to face
  immediate dismissal and being cut off from

working with others who are called to do God's work?

- Can you handle explosive anger from the family of the one with whom you had the affair? What if the anger gets out of hand?
- Can you handle the shame that will be brought to your family if you fail morally? The gossip, the criticism, the glances that make you wonder what people are thinking or saying?

"Honest with Myself"

Listen to the words of a man who thought he could handle it: "It took a personal 'world-shattering' event that was devastating, humiliating, and completely destructive to correct my path. It was not until I reached a point of being honest with myself that I could recognize my habit of choosing to place myself at points of temptation and make a turn toward a radical commitment to obey God, to deny myself, my desires, and my thoughts."

Did you notice his description of the consequences he had to face: world-shattering, devastating, humiliating, and completely destructive. Those are consequences I want to avoid at all costs. How about you?

- What if other couples who are now friends begin to distance themselves from you and your spouse? Even if your marriage survives your moral failure, your friends will never see you the same way.
- Are you ready to handle the long journey of confrontation, restoration, and healing? It won't happen overnight. In fact, it won't even happen in a few months. For the pleasure of the moment, you will spend the price of years.

If you're playing with temptation, you'll need a mega-calculator to count the cost of what you'll *really* have to handle.

Rationalization #2
"God Wants Me to Be Happy"

I'm amazed at how often I hear this statement. Yet when I hand my Bible to someone and say, "Show me where the Bible says that," I have yet to find anyone who can point to the Scripture claiming that God's primary goal for our life is to be happy.

Instead, God's Owner's Manual is clear that His primary desire for our life is that we be *holy*. What does that word mean in the twenty-first century?

It's not complicated. To be holy simply means to be set apart for a special relationship and service for God and to act accordingly. "Service" does not necessarily mean you must go into the ministry. It simply refers to the opportunity for God to use your life and mine in a special way to accomplish eternal things that will make an eternal difference in ourselves and others. Imagine that! You and I have the opportunity to experience a difference made by God in us, we can make a difference in others, and we can see those differences impact the future . . . even after we're gone. What a mind-blowing potential! And yet, many are willing to throw it away for a few moments of fun.

God calls us to be holy so that we can avoid tragic consequences and, instead, experience a personal relationship with Him and be usable by Him. In Leviticus 11:44, God challenges us to be holy: "I am the LORD your God; consecrate yourselves and be holy, because I am holy." In Hebrews 12:14, God says, "Make every effort to live in peace with all men, and to be holy; without holiness no one will see the Lord."

There it is again. God wants such a transforming change to take place in my heart that the resulting actions and attitudes in my life tell His whole story. And it's for my own good because here's what's ironic: He promises in His Word that if we strive to be holy, we inevitably will be happy. Yet if our focus is on being happy, we will rarely be holy.

One additional caveat—being holy is not about obeying rules, jumping through hoops, living up to somebody else's expectations, or having your name on a church's membership role. Being holy is having God so busy at work on our inner being that He's changing our want-to's. We *will* want to be different. We *will* want to act differently. We *will* want to have more biblical attitudes. And, we *will* want to follow God's Owner's Manual—to operate at maximum effectiveness and to avoid major breakdowns. The choice is ours. Preventive maintenance can go a long way!

Rationalization #3
"I Don't Want Anybody to Get Hurt"

I can't believe the number of people who've told me this in the midst of all their loved ones getting hurt. But I know one thing for sure: There's no such thing as a safe affair. I have yet to see the affair from which anyone walks away uninjured. More realistically, the shrapnel flies everywhere and wounds everyone in sight.

In the beginning of this book, I told you about a friend who had this very line of reasoning. I described him as brilliant off the chart. He'd played college football and started on a winning team. He was well liked and successful in his work. But, tragically, he was drawn into smut on the Internet. Finding pornographic site after pornographic site, he was sucked into the tangled web of sexual illusion, and his wife never had a clue.

But it didn't stop there. The porn sites led to the chat rooms. The chat rooms led to intimate discussions. Discussions led to invitations to meet. And a liaison led to an affair.

As his daughter turned nineteen and left for college and his son was fifteen, Brandt walked out on his family and his life. I well remember the devastation that happened just a year ago. The emotional shrapnel flew in all directions, and yet, amazingly, Brandt still believed that his relationships with the kids shouldn't have been affected at all. He E-mailed his nineteen-year-old daughter, saying that he really still loved her and wanted them to be close again—at least, in their hearts. Can you imagine this line of reasoning?

His beautiful daughter, heartbroken and shattered, responded to his E-mail. I shared a few sentences of it earlier in this book. If you think no one gets hurt, just take a moment, and read the E-mail in total:

> I cannot comprehend the sincerity of anything you say anymore, Dad. You say that you love me, yet you, knowingly, hurt both me and my family. You say that you would die for me, but you were unwilling to live for me. You say that you miss me, yet it is you who left and abandoned me. I am learning that words are a cheap commodity . . . especially, your words.
>
> I am angry with you for living a life of deception and for going against everything you have ever taught me to be true and right. I disrespect you as a man, a husband, and as a father. You are a coward for not being willing to sacrifice something for the love of your own children. More than anything, I

pity you. I pity you for throwing your life away for lust. You had every earthly thing a man could ever dream of: a loving family, two adoring children, a wonderful job, respect in our community, and all the possessions you could ever want. Yet you had a void in your life. Instead of filling that void with Christ, you allowed sin to fill it. You are caught inside a cloud of deception. I hurt for you because I know that one day, you will look back at your life and realize all that you lost . . . for nothing. And I am afraid for you because I know that God will deal with your sin in His time and that it will be far worse than any earthly punishment or grief you could encounter. You are in a dangerous position by not fearing the Lord.

I cannot allow you back into my life until you have a change of heart. As much as it hurts me to push you away, I believe that it is necessary for my healing. I don't believe that my brother and I are really a necessity in your life as you claim. I recall the many times, while growing up, that you convinced us that a parent could not desire anything more than love from his own children. Obviously, you have changed your mind—if you ever really meant those words in the first place. You seem to have no problem trading us for a replacement person. No matter how many times you say that you love me, I cannot believe the words without seeing the actions.

As disappointed and upset as I am, I will not cease to pray for you. I will pray that God will soften your heart. I will pray that you will not find the true peace or contentment until you are right with God. I will pray that one day, before we die, you will have a change of heart and lifestyle and that our relationship can be renewed. I will pray that, in time, God will grant me the grace to forgive you.

In the meantime, I will learn to live again. I will learn to trust and depend on the Lord to be my Father. I am thankful that God is a Father who will never betray, deceive or hurt me. Life will be different and difficult, at times, but I am confident that God will provide for Mom, my brother, and me. Each day will get a little easier and a little less painful to face.

Wow! And Brandt thought no one would ever be hurt. Do you have the same deception rolling around in your mind?

Rationalization #4
"You Just Don't Understand My Situation!"

Perhaps this is the most common deception of all. People think their circumstances are unique.

"It's different with me."

"If you had to deal with the spouse I have, you'd understand!"

"You don't know the stress I'm under. I've just got to have relief."

"I don't feel the love anymore like I used to."

"This person really understands me."

Do you know what's so amazing about all these statements and many more just like them? It's that, while people claim their situation is unique, they never use any unique reasoning. It's all the same old thing, just repeated by a different set of lips.

What are the answers to these rationalizations? Here are a few ways to face reality:

1. *Get honest.* There must be a willingness to confess and confront the issues and facts as they really are. Wrong has to be called "wrong," and sin has to be called "sin." While it may be an old term, it's an ever-present reality.

2. *Admit you need help.* One thing that's become obvious through the years is that someone can't be helped unless they feel they need it. You can't dance around the issues, because the issues are critical and life-threatening. There's no time for games.

3. *Make yourself accountable.* Invite into your inner life a few people who love you enough and are courageous enough to ask you the hard questions. People who can tell when you're putting on a front. People who

won't settle for answers like, "Everything is OK."
Remember, most often people will hold you accountable
only if you grant them the right to do so.

4. *Take the long view.* Getting on the other side of bad
choices isn't a casual stroll. Instead, it's more of a
marathon run, and you must be willing to pay the price
and take the time to get things back in order. But, trust
me, the run is worth it if you're willing to step up to the
plate, once and for all, and start the journey.

Can you imagine Joseph rationalizing a decision to
sleep with his boss's wife? The next time you're tempted
to rationalize or justify in order to cover your bad
choices, think again. Maybe the best choice is to face
reality.

9

Staying or Fleeing

As soon as Chad's wife pulled out of the driveway and headed to the grocery store, he knew the coast was clear. With a click of the mouse, he filled his computer monitor with mind-boggling images. But they weren't about sports or finances or vacation spots. Instead, Chad allowed a serpent to enter into the comfort, privacy, and familiar accessibility of his home.

It wasn't a rattlesnake that slithered through the grass and into the house, but its bite was just as poisoning. Chad had allowed Internet pornography to invade the security intended for his home.

He was so engrossed with what lay before his field of vision that he failed to hear his wife re-enter the house. Having forgotten the checkbook, she entered the study to retrieve it from Chad, only to be stunned—and then horrified. Chad, with a mixture of embarrassment and anger, saw the betrayal and horror spread across her face . . . an image that would be burned into his memory bank for months to come.

Chad had joined the ranks of more than 17.5 million others who are crowding the Internet highways to get cheap thrills that cannot satisfy, looking for elusive representations that no one can live up to.

Add to that the almost $1 billion of pay-per-view on-line content that's filled with adult material, and you have another rattler coming into the homes of millions. In 2000, the Hot Network penetrated more than sixteen million homes carrying explicit pornography with all its venom. Yet, amazingly, the number one complaint is that its content is not explicit enough!

In 1999, we saw a total of $18 billion worth of sales of cybersex videos and accessories to, primarily, home-based buyers.

Joseph and David were two different—and yet similar—men. Both were gifted. Both experienced tremendous success. People were drawn to both men and recognized their leadership qualities. Blessings seemed to accompany much of what they attempted, and both were, undoubtedly, men's men.

Yet one man guarded his heart; the other left his heart unguarded. And that made all the difference.

When Joseph's temptation sprang before him, the Bible says he was ready before the event ever occurred. Temptation requires that. If you're going to be able to

Guard Your Heart

Candy thought it strange that the pastor began dropping by while her husband was away. Warning bells sounded, but she dismissed them. *After all,* she reasoned, *if you can't trust someone in ministry, who can you trust?*

He was a sparkling conversationalist and seemed to take real interest in Candy, her family, and their lives. *If only my husband would act half as interested. His job is sucking every bit of his energy and attention.*

"Guard your heart, for it is the wellspring of life" (Prov. 4:23). Candy breathed a prayer that she would have the strength and conviction not to give in to any temptation that could have devastating effects on her family. Then something changed. She felt less comfortable when the pastor dropped by, and so she quit inviting him in. Not content just to visit her through the front door, he discontinued coming.

One day Candy's phone rang. Had she heard the news? Pastor so-and-so was confronted this morning about being involved in several affairs! Shocked, Candy returned the receiver to its cradle. The horror of the reality sunk in. Candy could have been one of those.

handle it, you'd better determine your course of action *before* the temptation comes knocking. When it knocks is no time to determine how you're going to respond.

But how do we guard our heart? Some principles . . .

Principle #1
Be Careful What You View

It's been said that the eyes are the windows to the soul. That being the case, it's critically important to monitor what goes in the eye because of its impact on the soul.

The oldest book in the Bible indicates an understanding of this principle. According to Job 31:1, Job made a covenant with God concerning his eyes, promising not to look with lust upon a young woman. Job understood that temptation often enters through the door of our sight. That's what Eve experienced when she looked upon the fruit and desired it.

Because of the importance of taking care with what we allow our eyes to view, let's consider the devastation that Internet pornography is bringing. Many are being lured into a tangled web of seduction both inside and outside the church. *Christianity Today* conducted an exclusive survey of its readership in August 2000. It was anonymous, which may explain why the answers were so honest. One-third of clergy responding and one-third of laypeople responding admitted that they had visited a sexually explicit Web site. Web surfers will expend more than $3 billion by 2003 on pornographic Web sites alone.

This lethal serpent that so many are allowing into the private confines of their homes and offices is successful because of:

- Twenty-four-hour accessibility
- Anonymity
- Immoral extremities
- Affordability
- Protected privacy

Unless you think that this is just an issue with men, research is now showing that women in the thirty-to-thirty-five-year age bracket are becoming more sexually aggressive. Experts say this is because they grew up in a much more visual society. These women are reaching an age when husbands may travel a great deal, and their children are at the age of exercising a great drain on the mother's energy. A good friend who leads a retreat center for couples experiencing trauma told me that a growing number of women at the empty-nest stage of life are being drawn to Internet pornography.

Remember that what you see is what you get! I encourage women everywhere I go to be careful about watching soap operas during the day or dramas at night that show more sexual encounters outside of marriage than inside. Also, be wary of romance novels. The descriptions you find in them would be impossible to live out in the reality of daily life.

Men need to be on guard for entry-point products, such as the *Sports Illustrated Swimsuit Edition* and when his wife receives the Victoria's Secret catalog. The best place in the world for both is the trash can. What your eyes do not allow to etch upon your brain, you won't have to worry about trying to erase. And moms and dads, please be careful of your children. Ted Roberts, in his outstanding book *Pure Desire*, tells us that the average age today for a first-time viewer of pornography is eleven. You're building a legacy!

Principle #2
Be Careful What You Think

It's been said that we can't always help what comes into our minds, but we have all the control in the world over what stays there.

Sounds easy, doesn't it? I've found in my journey that it's anything but. To dwell on the right things, especially when the wrong things are knocking at the mind's door, requires an incredible amount of discipline—every bit as much discipline as teaching your fingers to fly across the keyboard of a piano, or the discipline it takes to become an outstanding competitor in your favorite sport, or the discipline it takes to take off the extra twenty pounds that seem to jiggle with every step you take. None of those things just happens, and neither does the discipline of controlling your mind.

Watching Your Eyes

If you happen to be a man reading this, let me ask you a question. When you're out with your wife for dinner, and a beautiful woman (somewhat seductively dressed) enters the restaurant, what happens? Have you noticed that your wife's back can be to the door, but some God-given radar tells her what's just happened? The amazing thing is that, rather than turning around and looking at the woman who's just entered, your wife looks only one place. She watches your eyes to see where they will go.

In fact, Paul said that *transformation* is the only way thought patterns can become pure. The word itself refers to a literal change in nature that brings about a whole new quality. In Romans 12:2, Paul challenges us to become *transformed* in our minds. He's telling us that if we're going to be able to control our thoughts, we can't just do it with resolutions made from the outside in. Instead, it will only happen with transformation that moves from the inside out.

The only thing that can give us a brand-new nature inside is a personal relationship with God through Christ. Our Owner's Manual says that when we invite into our life the living Word (Jesus Christ, the full expression of who God is), we will develop a spiritual hunger for the written Word, and that's a key for transformation. Jesus was able to face temptation successfully, because His thought process was so grounded in the Word of God and He knew that, when temptation knocked, He would choose the will of God. Can you say that about yourself? That's what is meant in Psalm 119:11: "I have hidden your Word in my heart [thought processes] that I might not sin against you."

Principle #3
Be Careful What You Feel

In our day, it seems that emotion too often sits in the driver's seat of our lives. But can emotions be trusted? Many studies, both secular and sacred, prove that emotions are significantly unpredictable. Emotions can be affected by such a diverse range of conditions as the food we eat, the people we're with, the sleep we've had (or not had), the weather we're experiencing, and even the barometric pressure. How's that for a foundation for unpredictability!

Principle #4
Be Careful Where You Go

Our feet can take us in good directions and lousy directions. One of our most important choices is the friends with whom we walk. That's why Psalm 1 warns us about walking with the wrong crowd. Go back and re-read it. It cautions against an inevitable progression, warning us that—if we hang around with the wrong crowd—we'll move from an acquaintanceship with them to a fellowship among them to becoming absorbed as one of them.

Well, I know you're saying that you can handle that. Even though you may be hanging around some people with questionable values and habits, you're convinced you'll be a good influence on them. You feel that you'll raise the standard. You've convinced yourself that you'll be their savior. I wish I had a dollar for every time I've heard that. But I have yet to see it work! Are you going in the right direction with the right crowd?

Joseph knew how to handle each one of these issues. After he refused to go to bed with Potiphar's wife, he wouldn't even allow himself to be around her, day after day. If he wasn't around her, he didn't have to worry about being distracted or tempted to look at her body, fantasize in his mind, let his emotions get overheated, or the danger of hanging around someone with lower standards. Those very issues, combined with an obvious knowledge of God's Word and ways, enabled him to stand tall.

David, on the other hand, left his heart unguarded. Through the years I've studied many with whom I've walked through the tragedy of moral failure, and I've found there's an inevitable process:

Discontentment or anger. A person becomes discontented with his or her circumstances, spouse, or personal condition. It seems this often comes coupled with a deep-seated anger. While the anger may not be initially observable, it's inevitably present. This leads to an emotional openness and vulnerability.

Wandering eyes. Discontentment, regardless of the basis, coupled with anger can easily lead to being on a restless prowl. Members of the opposite sex catch the eye. And rather than glancing and going on, their eyes seem to be magnetically drawn and affixed on someone other than their own mate.

Wandering mind. When temptation enters the eyes, the mind goes into overdrive creating a fantasy. It can happen in a matter of seconds, yet leave a picture on the mental grid as clear as a two-hour movie. And the more the eyes wander, and the more the mind is allowed to fantasize, the more action is prompted.

Unintentional circumstances. When you're discontented and even a little angry and your eyes and mind are allowed to wander, it's only a matter of time until you find yourself with someone you believe can understand your pain. She is ready to listen. He seems to care. They're warm and receptive. It can happen at work or at church or some other social setting. You'll most likely see them in their best appearance, unlike those inevitable times when you see your spouse in his or her worst appearance. And you'll be tempted to take note that this is somebody you'd like to get to know a little bit better and with whom you'd like to spend more time.

Intentional circumstances. When the unintentional circumstances strike a chord deep inside, the other person may be drawn to fill the emptiness you feel. That feels comfortable, and so you begin to orchestrate ways to be around the person more often. You look for opportunities to experience a casual touch or an inadvertent bump. You find yourself being drawn to look deep into the eye, because, after all, the eye is the window to the soul. Excuses will be made. Justifications will be created. Fantasies will be born.

Intimate encounters. These will often begin with words. You'll find yourself complimenting or being complimented. Warmth will cloak the words that flow between the parties. A touch of hands will lead to the temptation to embrace the body—even quickly—and the public embrace will generate a desire for the private embrace. Then, the next thing you know, there's kissing and groping and . . . disaster.

Justifying and covering. Now the betrayal is complete. The damage has been done. The guilt has already begun. And the deed must be covered. And so the strategy forms of how to suppress the truth.

And so it was with David. Go back and read 2 Samuel 11 once more. Walk through each of these sequential steps, and you can see them in your mind's eye as David stood on the roof. Isn't it amazing? We don't fall into sin. We slide into it. One dangerous misstep on the slippery slope of temptation can lead to an avalanche of consequences.

When David finally heard that Bathsheba was pregnant, notice his immediate response. He began to scheme about how to justify his actions and cover his deed.

In hearing of love relationships that have degenerated, I've found an inevitable four-step sequence.

1. *Devotion.* They begin with a devotion characterized by a reckless abandonment of love. There's nothing you won't do for the one you love.

2. *Distraction.* But if you aren't careful, in time distraction sets in. Oh, it doesn't have to be distraction with bad things. It can be distraction with good things, such as church work that takes too much family time. But the more good things that get piled into life, the more you get drawn away from the reckless abandonment of the initial love relationship.

3. *Drifting.* If it's not caught and corrected, the inevitable next step is a drifting apart. Drifting is the beginning of a move away from sensitivity with which the love relationship began.

4. *Departure.* If the drift is not stopped and corrected, there's an inevitable departure. The departure, at first, may be emotional—but it's departure, nonetheless. And given enough time, it will, inevitably, become physical departure.

How many times have you and I seen this happen in the lives of people we know? People who, at one time, were radically in love with one another. But somewhere along the way, either good things or bad things or a combination of both began to distract them, and they didn't make the effort to catch the problem and correct it. They began to drift apart. And because the drifting was not stopped, eventually it led to departure.

Through my years as an executive in the business world and in ministry at various levels, I have dealt with scores of love relationships and marriages that started with an uncompromised devotion. But often, with the passage of time and with slipping of intentionality, distraction occurred. Oh, granted, it was often distraction with good things—children, jobs, two careers, hobbies, avocations, and even volunteer of church work. But, distractions, nonetheless. And if the love relationship isn't caught there and returned to devotion, it moves to drifting, and the drifting takes people apart. Rather than growing together, they drift separately. And if the alarms don't go off there, it leads to departure. First, emotional. And then, too often, physical.

Just look at the pattern, and think how many times you have seen it happen in the lives of people you know, or even in your own life.

DEVOTION ⇨ DISTRACTION ⇨ DRIFTING ⇨ DEPARTURE

This pattern is true in our personal, human relationships (horizontal), but it's also true in our spiritual relationship with God (vertical). In Deuteronomy 30:15–18, we see the same four-step reality of how our relationship with Him can begin with great strength and dissolve to tragic separation. Here are the four steps:

1. Love Me, the Lord your God, with all your heart, and you will be blessed in all you do.
2. Be careful lest you become distracted with other things or other people.
3. And if you become distracted long enough, you will begin to drift, and you will turn away from Me.
4. And if you turn away from Me very long, you will begin to worship other gods—that is, you will look to someone else or something else to fulfill your life as only I, the Lord your God, am able to do.

I believe that, if you're in danger of moving away from a reckless, abandoned love for God, you'll also be in danger of moving away from a reckless, abandoned love for your spouse. Before you read any further, do you need to take some corrective action? Do you need to return to your reckless, abandoned love for God? Or if you have never had one, why don't you tell Him right now . . .

Lord God, I need You. I understand that You have loved me with an everlasting love and in loving-kindness have drawn me to Yourself. You love me so much that You sent Your Son to die in my place, to pay for my sin.

At this very moment, I want to admit that I have become distracted. I want to get back to being focused on the right things. Restore in me the love for You, first, and the love for my spouse, second.

Please draw me back to Yourself, for I know that the closer I come to You, the closer I will come to my spouse. Keep me from trying to fill the God-shaped vacuum in my life with anything or anyone else.

Help me not to be nearly as concerned with trying to have the right mate as I am with trying to be the right mate.

Thank you for hearing my prayer.

Amen.

10

Leaving a Legacy of Tragedy or a Legacy of Triumph

Have you ever noticed that when you work for an organization, you have a desire to leave the organization better than you found it? In other words, you want it to improve or benefit as a result of your having been there?

In my family, the same could be said of any neighborhood in which we've lived, any church to which we've belonged, any social club in which we've been a part, or any friends with whom we've shared life. It's just an ingrained part of who we are.

In essence, we want to leave a *legacy*. We want to pass on something from our life that benefits those around us and those who follow us. It's that deep, abiding desire harbored in each of our hearts to contribute something that will outlast our presence.

That desire is especially prevalent when it comes to our children and family—children, grandchildren, and beyond.

As I look across today's landscape, I must say I'm shaken. The rate of divorce has increased significantly since the 1960s, often due to infidelity. What's more sobering is that today the rate of divorce is slightly higher among born-again Christians than among others outside the church.[1]

In addition, one out of every three children now under the age of eighteen is living with a single parent—80 percent of those are living with their mother. Forty percent of all single mothers have never been married.

And the 2000 U.S. Census was just as sobering. A report released on May 15, 2001, showed that households headed by an unmarried parent had increased 72 percent over the decade of the 1990s. Households headed by single mothers had increased 25 percent in the same time, and 62 percent when headed by fathers. For the first time in U.S. history, the family headed by two parents living together fell below the 25 percent mark in the population.

Regardless of the reasons, it's evident by watching the statistics of our land that we've sown to the wind, and now we're reaping the whirlwind. I'm praying that, if you're part of a wonderfully intact family, you'll commit to doing everything in your power to guard and grow your marriage and family. If, by chance, you have walked through the difficult days of a family rupture, remember that God is the God of a second chance. Rise up and teach your children the sanctity of marriage, and if there have been mistakes in your past, step up to the plate and admit them. That's what mature adults do. You'll grow strong in the eyes of your children, and their respect for you will deepen immensely. If we don't do this, it's our children and grandchildren who will suffer the consequences far more than even we ourselves.

Those who counsel marriages in crisis report that the vast majority of marriages break apart not suddenly, but by a creeping loneliness, boredom, or anger. It's the little things that build to become the seemingly unsolvable things. Small fissures below the surface of relationships, when not dealt with, become percolating and fiery volcanoes.

What can a couple do to work hard at growing a solid marriage and a stable home? I suggest that each couple go away for a two- or three-day escape and ask each other a series of questions. Obviously, what will determine the benefit of these questions will be the honesty with which they are answered. Try them, and see what happens.

Every husband should ask his wife . . .

- Do you know that I truly love you, and do I make it obvious? If not, what can I do to improve that?

- Do you feel that I express my love to you enough in front of the children so there's no question in their mind of my love for you? If not, how can I improve it?
- Am I treating you as the most important person on earth to me? What could increase that feeling in you?
- I promised to cherish you. Do you feel that way, and what could I do to strengthen that?
- What is your greatest concern about our family, and have you felt free to express it to me? If you've expressed it, have I listened?
- Do you feel that I'm helping you fulfill your God-given potential? How can I improve that?
- Am I doing anything that would ever lead you to be tempted to compromise in any area? If so, what could I do to change?
- Would you tell me your most significant dreams about the future?

In addition, every wife should ask her husband . . .

- Am I doing enough to make you feel adequate in our relationship and assuring you that I see you that way?
- I know it's important for you to feel honored and affirmed. Do I make you feel that way, and what can I do to improve?
- How can I help you best succeed at your work as you provide for the needs of our family?
- Do you feel that I know and understand what your greatest dreams are for the future?

- What could I do better to support your leadership in our family?
- Am I doing anything that would ever lead you to be tempted to compromise in any area? If so, what could I do to change?

Here are some questions that you may jointly share with each other and discuss.

- How do you feel we're doing in expressing our own personal faith as a living reality in front of our kids?
- Are we sometimes allowing our children to play one of us against the other, and if so, what adjustments do we need to make to avoid that?
- Are we praying for our children's future and for the mates God is preparing for them?
- Do our children understand that our marriage relationship is the priority in our family?
- How are we each doing individually and together as a couple on building our spiritual lives?
- Is the atmosphere of our home one that is filled with joy and expectation? If not, what adjustments need to be made?
- What are we doing to make sure that we are growing together, as opposed to growing apart?

The question may be crossing your mind, *Will these questions guarantee my marriage, our relationship, and the future of our family?* The answer is no. Nothing can guarantee that except your commitment, hard work, and the presence of God in your home. But it would start you down a long but important road—a journey that demands authenticity, vulnerability, flexibility, and integrity.

If you're one of those who was brought up to believe that a marriage that works is a 50–50 deal . . . forget it! Marriage that works is a 100–100 deal. It takes everything both partners have to give to make the home your children and your grandchildren deserve.

The decision you make about your willingness in this area will determine the legacy you leave. If you have any question about whether the choices we make—good and bad—affect our future generations, just read the statistics. Study how many kids who have been abused become abusers, who have grown up in alcoholic homes become alcoholics, who have grown up around promiscuity become promiscuous, who have lacked an environment of strong Judeo-Christian values grow up to be valueless. And just take a look at Joseph and David and the legacies they left.

Joseph

- Joseph ministered hope to a fellow prisoner in jail concerning his pending release, which came to reality.
- He helped Pharoah understand a God-given dream that would eventually save all of Egypt.

- He was made Egyptian prime minister, second only to Pharoah and, thus, positioned to help an entire nation.
- Joseph established a national food stockpiling and distribution plan to cover seven years of plenty followed by seven years of famine; it would be the salvation of Egypt.
- Joseph forgave his brothers, who had flagrantly abused him and sold him into slavery, when he had the chance to destroy them.
- Joseph saved the lives of his extended family and provided them with a new home in Egypt, where they survived.
- God used Joseph to perpetuate the nucleus of what would become the nation of Israel, God's chosen people.
- Joseph is one of the few men in the Bible about whom nothing negative is said.
- He would become a model for living life according to God's guidelines, not only in Israel, but across the world.
- God's hand was upon him and his family all the days of his life.

David

- The baby conceived illegitimately with Bathsheba died at birth.
- In attempting to cover his wrong, David had Bathsheba's husband killed.

- David's daughter, Tamar, was raped by his son, Amnon.
- Absalom murdered Amnon.
- Absalom rebelled against his father repeatedly, causing great heartache and an attempt to undermine his father's reign.
- Absalom purposely attempted to steal the hearts of the people of Israel from his father.
- Absalom incited rebellion against his father.
- Absalom seized David's throne and slept with some of David's wives.
- One of David's trusted generals killed Absalom in battle.
- David's grief over the tragedy of his son caused bitterness in the troops who had stood with David against Absalom.
- The trail of violence never left David's household all the days of his life.
- David's successor and son, Solomon, struggled with sexual addiction (seven hundred wives and three hundred concubines.)
- Solomon allowed many of his foreign wives to bring their false religions and practices with them, thus undermining the monotheism of Israel.
- At Solomon's death, the nation of Israel was split asunder.
- Israel's history was plagued with war after war.

1. George Barna, *Boiling Point* (Regal: Ventura, CA, 2001), 42.

11

Saying "I Don't" or
Saying "I Still Do"

So there you have it. Choices make all the difference! Plus a willingness to forgive even when you don't want to. To really believe that God's way is the best way. When temptation knocks, *not* to answer the door. And to honor the commitment to stand on conviction rather than comfort. These decisions—and more—can make all the difference. It's not just for now but for all the way to the finish line of life. A wonderful friend taught me this lesson.

Before my current position, I had the privilege and joy of pastoring a great church on the coast of Virginia at the Chesapeake Bay, First Baptist of Norfolk. While there, I met Bob. Bob was somewhat unemotional, yet he had a razor-sharp mind and a tremendously quick wit. By his own admission, sharing his softer side was

---

Foundation or Fault Line?

Just remember, every moment-by-moment choice places another solid brick in the structure of a marriage, creating either a firmer foundation or a fault line that will lead to collapse.

---

not his strength. That's why Bob's words about his wife made such an impact on me. First, some background.

Bob married Nan when he was twenty-one and she was eighteen. Like all couples, their marriage required adjustment and a great deal of give-and-take. Typical of task-oriented husbands, Bob was immersed in his work, and even as the children came along, he was absorbed in providing for the family and fulfilling his calling. His life was a series of moment-by-moment choices, and Bob made the ones that honored his marriage vows.

On the way to a restaurant one evening, the true richness of their relationship came exploding to the surface. Driving on a beautiful fall evening, Bob turned to Nan and said, "After all these years together, I'm still excited about taking you to dinner and having personal time with you. It's as though we're starting our relationship all over again as newlyweds. After all these years, I still do."

Nan lovingly turned to him from the passenger side of the car, and with a twinkle in her eye and a mischievous smile on her lips, goaded him with, "You must really be sick!" Then they both laughed.

In reality it was not Bob who was sick, but Nan. She had suffered a major stroke and later would experience multiple ministrokes, so when this conversation occurred they weren't young, passionate lovers whose words came easily and, sometimes, flippantly. No, Nan and Bob were veterans of *sixty-two years* of marriage.

Soon after this dinner Nan declined rapidly. She was no longer ambulatory. Bob had to care for her twenty-four hours a day, seven days a week, month after month.

As Bob watched his bride of so many years continue on a downhill slide, I grieved for him. One day following worship service, I spoke to him at the front of the church.

"Are you doing OK?" I asked. "Are you holding up?"

I was amazed that with a beaming smile as radiant as any face I've ever seen he replied, "Oh, yes! It's the greatest delight and joy of my life to minister to my wife and take care of her every need during these times. She's given so much to me through these years. Now it's my turn to give back to her!" And looking into his face, there was no question as to whether he meant it. I watched him care for her day in and day out, until—from massive heart failure—Nan died.

Bob taught me a great lesson about the success of a marriage. It's not how it starts, but how it finishes.

Granted, the beginning can be important because everything that's built on a solid foundation stands more solid for the duration of time. But inevitably in a marriage the winds of conflict will blow, the tremors of disagreement will shake, the storms of trouble will flood, and the crevices of disappointment and disillusionment will attempt to swallow the couple to the depths of failure.

I made a determination in my mind as I stood in front of the church that day with Bob. I want to end my life and my marriage at the finish line just like that! How about you? Did you mean it when you said, "In sickness and in health, for better or for worse, for richer or for poorer . . ."?

Are choices really that important? You bet!

Contrast Bob with another friend named Tony, who made different choices and the sad words he wrote to me:

> I had been married for over sixteen years and had three wonderful children. To confess accurately, I need to make clear that my biggest sin was not having an affair or committing adultery. My biggest sin was letting my marriage deteriorate so irretrievably.
>
> My former wife and I had been having problems almost since the beginning of our marriage . . . I have to take the blame for allowing the marriage to die. According to the Bible, I was to be the spiritual leader and, therefore, the buck stopped with me. It

died! I take responsibility for that . . . I have learned through this pilgrimage that I could have and should have done more to save my marriage. It did not happen. I believe the details of my failed marriage are not appropriate in this context. Suffice it to say that my biggest failure was letting my marriage die.

What Bob and Tony show in contrast is that choices make all the difference in life. They made the difference for Bob and Tony, for Joseph and David, and they will make the difference for you and me. Will we guard our hearts or not? What moment-by-moment choices will we make? Like Joseph and David, the answer will impact our world, not only for us, but also for our children and grandchildren. If your heart is guided by God, then I know you have what it takes to make the right ones.

12

Standing with Joseph or Falling with David

One of my favorite movies is *Three Men and a Baby*. Three very different men all trying to determine what they're going to do with a baby.

In this book, we've seen "two men and a temptation." Two different men determining what they were going to do when faced with the lure of temptation.

One recognized his weaknesses—the other overestimated his strengths.

One used his position responsibly—one irresponsibly abused it.

One guarded his heart—the other left himself wide open.

One determined to flee—one decided to stay.

One stood tall—the other fell flat.

Their moment-by-moment choices made all the difference in the world. So in closing I'll summarize the steps Joseph took that guided his life and led to the outcome I believe most of us want. The steps are found in James 4:7–10: "Submit yourselves, then, to God. Resist the devil, and he will flee from you. Come near to God and he will come near to you. Wash your hands, you sinners, and purify your hearts, you double-minded. Grieve, mourn and wail. Change your laughter to mourning and your joy to gloom. Humble yourselves before the Lord, and he will lift you up."

Joseph Submitted Himself Fully to God

Submission is an act of the will, not the emotions. To submit means to place yourself under the leadership of another and at that person's disposal. Joseph made the decision to place his life fully into the hands of God.

Joseph turned over the control room of his life. In fact, he invited God into that control room (his heart), and gave Him full and total access. No closets were off-limits; no rooms had locked doors. He gave God free reign in every area of his life.

Paul captured it powerfully in Romans 12:1–2: "Offer your bodies as living sacrifices, holy and pleasing to God—this is your spiritual act of worship. Do not conform any longer to the pattern of this world, but be transformed by the renewing of your mind." He compared committing our bodies to what many scholars believe was the burnt offering in the Old Testament. That offering was consumed by fire. Every part of it was surrendered, representing the life of the person offering the sacrifice, symbolically yielding all to God. Then God could lead where He knew was best, change anything that needed changing, take away anything that was a hindrance, and produce a life filled with joy, discipline, peace, and faith.

It also represented the one offering that symbolized the life of the offerer being placed at the disposal of God. He and his family were available to be used of God, however the Lord saw fit. The main issue could no longer be the individual's agenda, but God's.

Paul said we would be transformed from the inside out. The word *transformed* means "to be changed in nature." That's no mere New Year's resolution or weight-loss goal. The transformation brings a totally new temperament and life view. It is primarily accomplished by the individual getting into the Word of God. Even more, by the Word of God getting into the

Recognizing God's Will

A result of submitting ourselves fully to God is knowing what is God's will for our life, our family, and our future. And we'll recognize God's will because it will be good, never bad; it will be pleasing, never harmful; it will be perfect, never lacking.

individual. A whole new God-centered perspective results. And it requires our intentional decision to prevent the world around us from squeezing us into its mold, but instead, allowing God to renovate us from inside out.

Joseph Resisted the Devil

To resist is an action that doesn't just happen. It is intentional and focused. It means that when temptation comes knocking, we don't give it a second thought. We expect temptation to arrive, and we've made up our minds what we'll do: immediately resist and flee.

As we've learned through the journey of this little book, we're wise to prepare for any temptation as Jesus did—by knowing God's Owner's Manual so well that, when temptation comes knocking, we know what the Book says about how to respond. And, by knowing, we don't dialogue or debate; we just decide.

What an amazing result! The promise is that if we resist the devil, he will flee from us. He will go looking for those who won't resist him. Like a burglar who avoids homes with low-cut shrubbery, excellent lighting, alarm systems, and dogs, Satan avoids Christians who are prepared for his evil arrival.

Remember, the psalmist said to God, "I have hidden your word in my heart that I might not sin against you" (119:11). If we do that, the likelihood is far less that we will give in to temptation. But if we don't . . . !

Remember, it's a choice. "I have chosen the way of truth; I have set my heart on your laws" (Ps. 119:30). When Satan knocks and faith answers the door, you'll be amazed. You'll find no one there!

Joseph Drew Near to God

How can we do this? The same way we become closer to people in our own family. We spend time with them—quantity time and quality time. We communicate with them. We're an active and interactive participant. We speak, but we also listen. (And having two ears and one mouth, it's probably wise to listen twice as much as we speak.)

A few questions . . .

1. Do you pray daily, and when you pray, do you only talk, or do you also listen when you finish what you want to say to hear what God is saying?

2. Do you read a little of God's Word every day, or a devotional book that incorporates God's Word? That's a primary way He speaks to you.

3. Do you regularly attend an active church that believes the Bible means what it says and says what it means and is the fully revealed Word of God? If not, why don't you find a church this Sunday?

4. When you go to church, do you actively participate in the worship, or are you a passive observer? It's hard

to draw near if you're passive. God wants a relationship with us that's interactive.

5. Do you pray with your spouse or fiancé? He or she will be the most important person (and because of pride, sometimes the most difficult person) you ever pray with.

6. Are you asking God:

- What do you want to change in me today?
- What do you want to teach me today?

When we take the initiative to draw near to God, the promised result is that He will draw near to us. You can't find a better promise than that!

The amazing thing about a marriage is that it is much like a triangle. Picture a triangle with God at the pinnacle and the husband and wife at the two bottom base

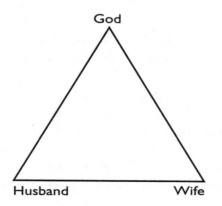

angles. Notice that—as the husband and wife become closer to God (moving up the sides of the triangle)—they, inevitably, get closer to each other.

But what if you've already blown it? Regardless of who was at fault, things fell apart. What if you identify with David, and you've made a mistake you wish you could erase? Is there hope?

Sure, there is.

James challenges us to wash our hands and purify our hearts. What does he mean? He means to confess our sin and repent. Those are Bible words, and your question may be, "What do they mean in the twenty-first century?" Let me help you.

To *confess* means to agree with God that what we've thought or done is outside His parameters according to His Owner's Manual (the Bible). We admit that it's what the Bible calls sin, meaning to miss the mark of God's guidelines, much like an arrow can miss the target for which it was intended. But, by confessing, we're agreeing with God that what we've done, felt, or thought is wrong.

To *repent* means to experience a change of mind and heart that leads to a change of direction. It means that we change our mind from insisting on doing things our way to doing things God's way (even if God's way is contrary to our way of thinking), because the change in mind will lead to a change in heart—and a new way of life. It means making a U-turn and charting a new course—God's course, according to His Word.

Oh, and one final but essential step: James says we must humble ourselves. Notice he doesn't say that God will humble us; it's a choice and an action that *we* must make. Humble people are the only ones in whom God can work.

So maybe you've got some choices to make. Or someone you know has some choices to make. My prayer is that the choices made will be the right ones—and that can make all the difference.

If you question that, just think back over the lives of Joseph and David, and then decide which course you want to follow.

God bless you as you guard your heart in this unguarded world.

13

When the Vow Breaks

Ruptured marriages. Broken hearts. Sexual infidelity. Shattered trust.

Who hasn't seen (or experienced) these tragedies in our families, friends, neighbors, and work associates? Some people survive spiritually; many do not. What makes the difference?

This book has addressed prevention. I would be remiss if I didn't address the appropriate Christian response to this problem when it does surface—even among our leaders.

Moral failures—like other problems such as addiction—are family tragedies that cause a ripple effect throughout the community associated with the person who fell. Obviously, spouses and children experience broken hearts and shattered trust, and people outside the family are shocked, their confidence shaken. But if the person is a Christian, the fallen person's community includes fellow believers—the body of Christ with the church at its center.

Society, of course, often shrugs when infidelity rears its ugly head above the water's surface, saying: "That's life. No big deal. It's none of my business." The other extreme is the response of too many Christians and churches: condemnation and isolation, which is why we're often accused of shooting our wounded.

But there's a better—and certainly more effective—way to respond, especially when we as the church recognize that "our wounded" includes those drowning spouses, children, friends . . . and fellow church members. Cheryl and I saw this recently when a Christian leader abandoned his family due to an adulterous affair. His teenage kids were shattered, yet their faith remained intact because they observed how their church responded. First, the church extended love and support to the wife and kids. And then they prayerfully considered church discipline that might result in restoration of the marriage and family—tough love, if you will, rather than a condemning spirit.

Here's what the church leaders did: They confronted the husband-father who was in the affair. He did not respond. Then they requested a meeting with him, but he refused. As a result, they felt they had no choice under the congregation's Bible-based policies and injunctions but to dismiss him from membership. The church handled each step of discipline biblically throughout the process, even to the point of gracefully approaching several church members who were somewhat supportive of the man and pointing out their responsibility to distance themselves from him due to his unrepentant spirit, according to 1 Corinthians 5.

Watching how all this unfolded made a huge impact on this man's kids as they saw the church maintain its biblical standards—with thoroughness and grace—and as they learned that there are consequences for sin in the church community. Without this lesson these teenagers might have compounded the problem by following in their father's footsteps down the slippery slope of sexual immorality. Instead, I expect they learned lessons that will stay with them as they mature, and I anticipate they will remain in the church community.

A Word to Church Leaders

The Bible makes clear that moral infidelity is to be confronted within the context of a local congregation or ministry. The approach is never to be one of condemnation and vicious criticism but one that encourages those involved to step forward, take responsibility, express genuine repentance, and enter a process of restoration: "Brothers, if someone is caught in a sin, you who are spiritual should restore him gently. But watch yourself, or you also may be tempted. Carry each other's burdens, and in this way you will fulfill the law of Christ" (Gal. 6:1–2).

The word *brothers* tells us this is written to Christians. The original language for the phrase "caught in sin" focuses on guilt that's provable (as opposed to reacting to rumor or someone's "feeling" that the person is committing sexual immorality). Notice the passage's emphasis on gentle (careful) restoration. The word translated "gently" literally refers to the mending of a torn fishing net or the setting of a broken bone. We know that the medical practice of setting a broken bone, though painful, is necessary for the bone to heal. Although it may cause pain, the doctor does not set it harshly but gently and firmly. The passage also tells us to "bear one another's burdens." This is written in present tense, indicating an ongoing process. In other words, restoration does not happen quickly and often not easily. In fact, I find it's much easier to condemn than to restore.

So, when a report of infidelity arises within the church community, it's crucial for the leaders to know as many facts as possible to determine if the report is true. With this information they must confront those involved. People holding leadership roles in the congregation (staff member, Sunday school teacher, choir member, etc.) should be removed from their responsibilities immediately, because leaders in ministry, whether vocation or laity, are instructed to "set an example for the believers in speech, in life, in love, in faith and in purity" (1 Tim. 4:12). And, while recognizing that church leaders must set an example and therefore be held to a higher standard, the church also should bear in mind that visionary leaders inevitably will attract critics and sometimes encounter false accusations. Perhaps for this reason Paul cautioned Timothy that he should never receive an accusation against a church leader unless confirmed by two or three witnesses (1 Tim. 5:19).

What if such disciplinary actions aren't taken in a loving but firm way by the church? The message to those watching is that the Word of God isn't really important nor are the Bible's truths absolute if church leaders don't appear to be taking them seriously or acting upon them.

Matthew 18:15–20 gives guidelines for confrontation. I love what David Augsburger says in his book *Caring Enough to Confront*. He makes the point that, if we really care about someone with a biblical love, we have no choice but to confront when significant sin arises. He challenges us to confront with care (love and compassion). In fact, he replaces the word *confronting* with *care-fronting*.

If you are a church leader who is called upon to confront a fellow believer carefully, remember to "watch yourself, or you also may be tempted" (Gal. 6:1). There is no room in confrontation for pious judgmentalism or an attitude of superiority.

The Goal of Biblical Confrontation

The ideal result when sexual immorality is confronted is that the involved parties take responsibility, repent, and commit to a process of restoration. Let's look at all three.

First, in taking responsibility, they must not point fingers in other directions or blame people and circumstances for their affair or indiscretion. People who genuinely step up to the responsibility admit that the immoral act was no one's fault but their own. In this day when so many people claim to be victims, it's much easier to blame something or someone else for our failures.

Second, genuine repentance is more than saying, "I'm sorry." People who say that can literally mean they were sorry for being caught, sorry for the inconvenience and embarrassment it has caused, sorry that they weren't more careful. Genuine repentance has at least three elements:

- I am wrong, and I have sinned (Ps. 51:3–4).
- I am sorry, and I want to make a 180-degree turn (Prov. 28:13).
- I desire forgiveness and want to be clean (1 John 1:9).

The Bible is clear that there is both superficial repentance and biblical repentance. In 2 Corinthians 7:10 we learn that superficial repentance accomplishes nothing, and, in fact, kills certain parts of us inside—our conscience, our sensitivity, and our ability to trust and be trusted. Biblical repentance leads to deliverance from the tragedy and leaves us with no regrets.

Third, the process of restoration is not quick, and it's not easy. A person who has been unfaithful can't just say "I'm sorry," turn over a new leaf, and expect there to be no consequences. While forgiveness can be granted immediately, trust has to be rebuilt. And that's because trust was shattered by the parties involved in the affair who were living a lie—lying to themselves, lying to those around them, and lying to God. Lying always destroys trust.

Rick Warren, who pastors Saddleback Community Church in California, says: "Forgiveness is immediate, but restoration after adultery always takes time. I have found in more than thirty years of public ministry that it takes at least a year. And it takes deep and very painful growth."

Author Tim LaHaye says: "The shortest period I am familiar with for [restoration from] adultery is two years, and it could go as high as five."

Some people take the position that anyone who commits adultery while serving in vocational ministry can never be restored to the point of serving in that professional calling again. Each church, ministry, or denomination must work through this issue and come to a conclusion they believe is biblical. But whether ministers ever return to vocational ministry is not as important as whether they are restored to God and to their spouse.

People who fall morally would be greatly helped by a church-appointed restoration team of two or three godly, mature, and caring members of the congregation who are the same gender as the person seeking restoration. The team's role should be walking alongside through a process of support, prayer, Bible study, and accountability. Mature help is essential for getting on one's feet again spiritually, emotionally, and relationally.

And we must not forget about the families of those who have failed. The innocent family members also need help from the church and its ministries in working through the issues and rebuilding their lives and relationships. Bible-based counseling should be provided for all affected by the shipwreck of infidelity.

I recommend counseling based on the Bible and its principles because I've found that psychotherapy may provide secular perspective but does not result in biblical restoration. Secular-based psychology alone does not heal spiritual wrongs and wounds. The wronged spouse, in particular, will have much anger, fear, and possibly bitterness to resolve and forgive. In my book *Forged by Fire* I dealt extensively with these issues and how successfully to overcome difficult times, including God's process of forgiving and moving on.

In my journey I've found that, when marriages need to be rebuilt, the best setting is a Bible-centered marital counseling retreat. These retreat centers exist around the country and can be a tremendous aid to couples seeking restoration. They enable the shattered couple to step out of their normal routine and into a private, focused setting to attempt to rebuild the broken pieces.

In summary, it's critical for the church to fulfill its role to prevent sexual immorality by providing clear biblical teaching and an unapologetic doctrine supporting the sanctity of marriage. And if indiscretion does occur within the ministry or the membership, the church must address it with compassion and biblical discipline with the goal of seeking restoration for those involved, so that life and love might be rebuilt.

Resources

Books

Arterburn, Steven, Fred Stoeker and Mike Yorkey. *Every Man's Battle: Winning the War on Sexual Temptation One Victory at a Time.* Colorado Springs, Colo.: WaterBrook Press, 2000.

Carder, Dave. *Torn Asunder: Recovering from Extramarital Affairs.* Chicago: Moody Press, 1995.

Exley, Richard. *Deliver Me.* Nashville: Thomas Nelson, 1998.

Ferguson, David, Teresa Ferguson, Chris Thurman, and Holly Thurman. *The Pursuit of Intimacy.* Nashville: Thomas Nelson, 1993.

Hart, Archibald D. *The Sexual Man.* Nashville: Word Publishing, 1995.

Lewis, Robert and William Hendricks. *Rocking the Roles: Building a Win-Win Marriage.* Colorado Springs, Colo.: NavPress, 1999.

MacDonald, Gordon. *Rebuilding Your Broken World.* Nashville: Thomas Nelson, 1990.

Means, Marsha. *Living with Your Husband's Secret Wars.* Grand Rapids: Fleming H. Revell, 1999.